# Dramatic Sketches From Romans

*Robert Alan Ward*

CSS Publishing Company, Inc., Lima, Ohio

DRAMATIC SKETCHES FROM ROMANS

*To my friend and mentor
Pastor Jeremiah Riffe —
who planted within me the
idea of writing Christian drama*

Copyright © 2000 by
CSS Publishing Company, Inc.
Lima, Ohio

All rights reserved. No part of this publication may be reproduced in any manner whatsoever without the prior permission of the publisher, except in the case of brief quotations embodied in critical articles and reviews. Inquiries should be addressed to: Permissions, CSS Publishing Company, Inc., P.O. Box 4503, Lima, Ohio 45802-4503.

All scripture quotations are from the *New American Standard Bible*, copyright 1960, 1962, 1963, 1968, 1971, 1972, 1973, 1975, 1977 by the Lockman Foundation. Used by permission.

ISBN 1-7880-1343-2          PRINTED IN U.S.A.

# To The Pastor And The Drama Director

These dramatic sketches have been designed primarily to prepare a congregation to hear their pastor's messages moving through the book of Romans. They can, however, also be used as a resource for youth groups, Sunday school classes, outreach programs, touring drama groups, or other special occasions. As Romans covers nearly every aspect of Christian doctrine and life, so these vignettes can be used as a wide variety of settings.

Several words floated about in my mind as I composed these sketches:

**Biblical** — Believing the Bible to be the inspired word of God, I have tried to be faithful to its teaching as best I can understand it. These vignettes amount to my endeavor to parablize the principles taught throughout the book.

**Balance** — Balance keeps us from getting out of proportion in our thinking and demeanor. Though all biblical subjects are serious, we humans cannot live always on the somber side of things. I have tried to balance solemnity with humor, and to keep it in good taste.

**Variety** — Variety keeps us from becoming predictable and promotes an air of anticipation in an audience. All manner of subjects, situations, skills, people, and acting styles are called for in these sketches. Variety also gives the maximum number of people a chance to serve, and keeps the actors challenged, motivated, and having fun.

I do not claim to have covered everything in the book of Romans. Who can make such a claim? It might be better not to use drama every week. Do other things in between. Keep each week fresh and new — and Holy Spirit led.

**Entertaining** — These vignettes are meant to be entertaining. Let's face it. We all enjoy being entertained, and pay more attention, and are more likely to remember what has entertained us.

**Life-changing** — The purpose is to help change our lives in the direction of "the unity of the faith, and of the knowledge of the Son of God, to a mature man, to the measure of the stature which belongs to the fullness of Christ" (Ephesians 4:13). Thus they are meant to be encouraging where needed — or building, or teaching, or convicting as the case may be.

**Facilitating** — They are meant to lead naturally into the pastor's message. If they serve to help the pastor communicate the biblical text, they will have fulfilled their main purpose.

A section of follow-up questions is included at the end of each vignette. If these vignettes are used in capacities other than as sermon forerunners, the questions will be found useful for discussion times afterward. The pastor also might find them helpful in formulating the messages. I strongly recommend that he or she have a copy of this work.

I sincerely hope that all who are involved in producing these sketches find them enjoyable, enlightening, challenging, and life-changing. May God richly bless your efforts to serve him.

Robert Alan Ward

# Table Of Contents

|     | **Title** | **Theme** | |
|-----|-----------|-----------|----|
| 1.  | **The Cemetery** | *Resurrection of Christ* | 7 |
| 2.  | **The Secret** | *Sharing the gospel* | 11 |
| 3.  | **Suppressing The Truth** | *Two contrasting world views* | 13 |
| 4.  | **The Newcomer** | *Judging others* | 17 |
| 5.  | **The Fishing Pond** | *Temporal versus eternal* | 21 |
| 6.  | **The Room Of Death** | *Blindness to the gospel* | 25 |
| 7.  | **The Club** | *Salvation through faith alone* | 29 |
| 8.  | **The Interview** | *Faith begets perseverance* | 31 |
| 9.  | **The Soccer Team** | *Perseverance in hard times* | 33 |
| 10. | **The Plague** | *Humankind's helplessness* | 37 |
| 11. | **Whose Slave Are You?** | *One master or another* | 39 |
| 12. | **Poison** | *The wages of sin is death* | 41 |
| 13. | **The New Creation** | *Redemption through Christ* | 43 |
| 14. | **The Head Case** | *Flesh cannot resist sin* | 49 |
| 15. | **The Dam** | *Daily victory over sin* | 53 |
| 16. | **A Little Pain** | *Pain forgotten in heaven* | 57 |
| 17. | **The Prom** | *All works together for good* | 61 |
| 18. | **The Marionette** | *Man knows better?* | 65 |
| 19. | **Mommy's Birthday** | *Zeal without knowledge* | 69 |
| 20. | **The School Play** | *Salvation for the Gentiles* | 73 |

| | | | |
|---|---|---|---|
| 21. | **The Task** | *God's way or man's — not both* | 77 |
| 22. | **The Flower** | *Be what God made you to be* | 79 |
| 23. | **Getting Even** | *The folly of revenge* | 83 |
| 24. | **The Alaskan Cruise** | *Christians and government* | 87 |
| 25. | **The Donut** | *Accountability* | 89 |
| 26. | **Differences** | *Appreciating our differences* | 93 |
| 27. | **The Table** | *Unity in the body* | 97 |
| 28. | **The Pacesetters** | *Reaching out to the different* | 101 |
| 29. | **The Receptionist** | *Honoring faithful servants* | 105 |
| 30. | **The Bully** | *Victory over the enemy* | 109 |

**Piano music for Sketch 13 — The New Creation**     112

**Piano music for Sketch 18 — The Marionette**     115

**Piano music for Sketch 22 — The Flower**     116

# 1. The Cemetery

*Who was declared the Son of God with power by the resurrection from the dead, according to the spirit of holiness, Jesus Christ our Lord.* — Romans 1:4

The resurrection of Jesus Christ from the dead is an utterly essential doctrine of the Christian faith. If Christ is not risen, our faith is vain.

But has the fact of the resurrection become "old hat" to many of us? What would it be like to be introduced to this truth for the first time?

---

**Characters:**
Amnesia
Curator

**Setting:**
A cemetery. Perhaps fifteen headstones are set up throughout the stage, all with their inscriptions facing away from the audience.


(*Amnesia enters and looks about. He appears bewildered. Curator enters*)

**Curator:** May I be of some assistance, sir?

**Amnesia:** Is this the cemetery of the most famous people who have ever lived?

**Curator:** That is correct. What can I do for you?

**Amnesia:** They tell me I had an accident two years ago. I've been in a coma until just recently. Now I'm okay except that I have amnesia. I can't remember anything or anyone before the accident.

**Curator:** So you've come here to see if some of these famous names might jar your memory?

**Amnesia:** Partly. But the real reason is to get some inspiration. You see, I have no beliefs, no opinions, no prejudices; I don't know my purpose. So I thought I'd see how some of these famous people lived, and find someone to emulate.

**Curator:** Well, I'll be glad to show you around. This is the grave of Napoleon Bonaparte.

**Amnesia:** (*Reading the epitaph*) "I am no ordinary man, and the laws of propriety and morals are not applicable to me." Rather a proud man, it would seem.

**Curator:** He was a great military leader for the nation of France. In his day he conquered most of Europe.

**Amnesia:** So because of him, France rules Europe?

**Curator:** Well, no. He was eventually defeated and banished to a small, bleak island in the middle of the Atlantic Ocean called Saint Helena. There he died of cancer at 51 — alone — the rest of the world gladly rid of him.

**Amnesia:** What about this man, Charles Darwin?

**Curator:** He wrote a book called *The Origin of the Species*, which explains how life evolved from primordial slime to modern humans through natural selection.

**Amnesia:** What did that do for all of us?

**Curator:** Two men greatly influenced by his book were Karl Marx, who developed a system called Communism, and Adolf Hitler, who was the main driving force behind a movement called Nazism. Together, those two ideologies have been responsible for the murders of millions of people. Now, even though both of those ideas have largely fallen out of favor, other applications of his book control the thought processes of our culture today.

**Amnesia:** Probably bringing the same kinds of results. Have you got anyone around here who did something a little more constructive?

**Curator:** Here's Babe Ruth. Probably the greatest baseball player who ever lived.

**Amnesia:** What kind of a man was he?

**Curator:** Boisterous, profane, vain — a womanizer. As great as his baseball accomplishments were, they would have been far greater if he had had a little more self-control.

**Amnesia:** Still not what I'm looking for. What about this man — John Lennon.

**Curator:** He was the main genius behind a singing group called The Beatles.

**Amnesia:** Were they popular?

**Curator:** Probably the most popular singing group of all time. In fact, Mr. Lennon once said, "We're more popular than Jesus."

**Amnesia:** Jesus? I've seen that name around here.

**Curator:** Oh, yes, over here. Probably the most influential person who ever lived.

**Amnesia:** What a minute. Why is his grave empty?

**Curator:** Don't know. It's the only one like that around here.

**Amnesia:** (*Reading the epitaph*) "My sheep hear my voice, and I know them, and they follow me; and I give eternal life to them, and they shall never perish; and no one shall snatch them out of my hand."

**Curator:** Beautiful, poetic words. Now if you'll look over here ...

**Amnesia:** (*Never looking away*) Where can I find out more about this man?

**Curator:** There's a place called (*name of your church*) down the road a bit. The people there might be able to help you.

**Amnesia:** Thanks. See you later. (*Leaves quickly*)

**Curator:** You're welcome. Have a nice life. (*He exits the other way*).

## Discussion Questions:

1. Do you think it would be easier to speak about Jesus to someone who has never heard of him, or to someone who knows something about him, but is not a believer?

2. What are some of the things Jesus offers that none other can match? What qualifies him to offer these things?

3. If Jesus offers all these things, why do so many reject him?

# 2. The Secret

*For I am not ashamed of the gospel, for it is the power of God for salvation to everyone who believes, to the Jew first and also to the Greek* — Romans 1:16

What is there to be ashamed of? We have the words of eternal life. We who know Christ will spend eternity in heavenly fellowship with our God who loves us, and with the saints of all the ages.

Those who do not know Christ have an eternity of hatred, pain, fear, anger, and death to look forward to. This world is the best they will know and the worst we will experience.

So why all the timidity in telling others about Christ? None of us likes rejection. Many of us don't think our lives match our profession. The world constantly bombards us with the message that we mustn't "force" our views on others.

But this world is desperately lost without Christ, and we have received from our Lord the Great Commission to bring the message of salvation to every person. Maybe we need to learn from the well-known commercial: "Just do it."

---

**Characters:**
James
Wendy


**Wendy:** James, I'm healed! The doctor says my cancer is completely cured! Thank you for giving me the cure!

**James:** Always glad to help a friend.

**Wendy:** Now that your cure has saved me, I'm sure you'll be telling everyone about it.

**James:** Come again?

**Wendy:** You're going to tell everyone about this, aren't you?

**James:** You've got to be kidding. People will have to change their lifestyles. Who am I to tell others how to live?

**Wendy:** But this is the medical breakthrough of the century! It's a matter of life and death for millions!

**James:** That's their problem. Nobody's going to call me a freak.

## Discussion Questions:

1. If you had the cure for cancer, would you tell the world about it?

2. If the cure for sin and death is so much better than the cure for cancer, why do we hesitate to tell others of salvation through Christ?

3. Why do some reject the message of salvation?

4. What are some things we as a group can do to introduce others to a saving knowledge of Jesus Christ?

# 3. Suppressing The Truth

*For they exchanged the truth of God for a lie ...*          — Romans 1:25

    The following sketch covers the passage from Romans 1:18-25. The setting is an ancient kingdom that has no experience of God except from what can be seen. Solon's thought process is that of a heathen with no knowledge of God, who nevertheless wants to know his creator. Malwich, by contrast, has adopted the thought process of verses 21-23.

    These are essentially the two main world views vying for supremacy in our culture today. The Christian world view begins with God; the humanist with nature. Is man a moral creature, responsible to God and others for his actions, or is he the amoral product of his environment who cannot be blamed for doing what comes naturally?

    Within a culture the two views beget radically different results. When the Christian world view is dominant in a society, the results will be order and freedom. The humanist view appears to offer the greater freedom (we can do whatever we want) but always leads to chaos and confusion, which inevitably brings tyranny.

---

**Characters:**
King Roderick
Solon
Malwich

**Setting:**
An ancient kingdom long before the time of Christ.


*(King Roderick is on his throne. His two advisors enter from opposite directions)*

**King Roderick:** Men, something must be done. My whole kingdom is falling apart. Crime is rampant. Disease is out of control. Families are disintegrating. Everything is in chaos. The people are afraid — and angry. What should we do about it? Solon?

**Solon:** We need a uniform set of laws for everyone to agree upon and abide by.

**Malwich:** Ha! And whose laws are these?

**Solon:** If there were a being of superior wisdom than ourselves who gave us his laws, rewarded us for following them, punished us for flaunting them, and whom we honored as such — we would have an orderly society.

**King Roderick:** Does such a being exist?

**Solon:** Your majesty, I have thought much about this. I believe that he does. And I believe that, save for his might and for our vices, he is like us.

**Malwich:** (*Sneeringly*) How would you know?

**Solon:** There is one God because there appears to be one plan in creation. Everywhere I see order — the evidence of one intelligent design. His creation appears to be limitless in energy, so he must be more powerful still. And as we cannot see the end of the universe, I conclude that he is eternal and infinite.

**King Roderick:** But none of this speaks of a morality.

**Solon:** Ah, but it does. If he made us, I would logically assume that he knows better than we, how we should live. He would want us to live in keeping with his character. He is trustworthy and consistent. Night follows day as day follows night. Spring follows winter. Always it is the same. I assume that he would want us to be as reliable toward one another as he is toward us. And what is the greatest instinct within us?

**King Roderick:** The will to survive, and to preserve our species.

**Solon:** Truly. The problem is that when we apply it to ourselves individually, we act in ways that destroy us collectively. If this God has given us life — and the will to preserve it — we ought to respond in a way that desires the welfare of others, as well as for ourselves. I believe the word would be love. If I am loving others, I will not take their lives or their property. Rather, I will help them. If they treat me the same way, because they honor the same God, we can work together for the benefit of all. That is what will produce an orderly and free society. And everything we can observe points to the existence of just such a creator.

**Malwich:** No such creator exists.

**King Roderick:** Why not, Prince Malwich?

**Malwich:** A free society, Solon? Such a being would impugn upon our freedoms. Can one enjoy life if he must constantly submit to the restrictive will of some all-powerful ogre? Solon speaks in immaterial abstracts. We should look to seeable, knowable nature for our laws. A lion is least dangerous when he is fed. We must provide for everyone's needs. Then no one will need to steal or kill for them. We are not creatures beholden to some all-powerful being. We are products of the environment around us. Improve the environment and you will improve society.

**Solon:** My distinguished colleague, your opposition to the laws of a superior being does not preclude his existence. We are here. Our presence logically demands his existence. Nothing makes itself.

**Malwich:** I do not see this God.

**Solon:** Is it because he does not exist, or because you do not wish him to exist? Your majesty, it is up to you which of us you will heed.

## Discussion Questions:

1. Draw a line down the center of the chalkboard. At the top of one side write "Humanist World View." On the other side write "Christian World View." Have the audience brainstorm the contrasts and write them down on each side. Here is what a finished product might look like: (don't limit them to this)

   | **Humanist World View** | **Christian World View** |
   |---|---|
   | Begins with nature | Begins with God |
   | Man decides right and wrong | God decides right and wrong |
   | We must save ourselves | Only Jesus can save us |
   | We are amoral products of our environment | We are moral creatures responsible for our actions |
   | Death is the end of us | After death comes judgment |
   | There is no absolute truth | God is truth |

2. What kind of society will the humanist world view produce?

3. What kind of society will the Christian world view produce?

4. How is the "freedom" of a "no restraints" humanism really bondage?

5. How is the "slavery" of belonging to Jesus Christ really freedom?

# 4. The Newcomer

*For in that you judge another, you condemn yourself; for you who judge practice the same things.*
— Romans 2:1

Judgmental people invariably have one trait in common. They do the very things they judge others for — and seem totally oblivious to it. Among other things, sin begets blindness.

What is the difference between a judgmental spirit and a discerning spirit? The former seeks to raise itself by lowering others. It is destructive in its motivation and outcome. The latter comes from a heart that seeks to build, to protect, and to heal. Those with a discerning spirit are acutely aware of their own shortcomings. Such individuals criticize infrequently, and only with good reason.

---

**Characters:**
Francie
Harriet
Edwina
Cash register clerk

**Setting:**
A drug store. Have a long table set up halfway between center stage and stage left as the checkout counter.

*(The Clerk is on the end nearer the exit with something resembling a cash register. Francie and Harriet are putting their items on the counter for purchase. Edwina is shopping on the other side of the stage)*

**Francie:** Look, Harriet, there's Edwina. She's new to our Sunday school class. Let's invite her to go with us on our class trip to the botanical gardens tomorrow.

**Harriet:** No way, Francie. She's a gossip.

**Francie:** Really? How do you know?

**Harriet:** Well, Mabel told me that Thelma told her that she used to know a friend who knew someone who used to know her when she was Queen of the Asparagus Festival a few years ago — who said she was a gossip.

**Francie:** That's terrible!

**Harriet:** Yes, and I don't know how to say this but (*Pause*) she's also a liar and a cheat.

**Francie:** I had no idea. She seems so nice.

**Clerk:** Let's see now. A fly swatter, denture cream, Milk of Magnesia, one copy of *Muscle Magazine*, and a yo-yo. Will that be all?

**Harriet:** Yes.

**Clerk:** Sixteen thirty-three, please. (*Harriet hands her a twenty*) Out of twenty. (*Clerk hands Harriet some coins*) Sixteen, (*Clerk hands her some ones*) seventeen, eighteen, nineteen, and twenty. Thank you and come again.

(*Edwina, who has been browsing about, now comes to the counter with her purchase. She sees the other women just as they are leaving*)

**Edwina:** Oh, hi, ladies. I'm kinda new to the group and want to get to know people. Is there any kind of social activity going on this weekend?

**Harriet:** No.

**Francie:** Not next weekend either. We hardly ever do anything.

**Edwina:** (*A little taken aback*) Oh, well, it was good seeing you.

**Harriet:** (*Brushing her off*) Likewise — 'Bye.

(*Harriet and Francie get out of earshot of Edwina and the Clerk*)

**Harriet:** See what I mean about her?

**Francie:** Yeah. Say, didn't the checker give you one dollar too much in change?

**Harriet:** Yeah. She ought to be more careful.

(*They exit. Edwina exits a few seconds later. Then the Clerk exits*)

## Discussion Questions:

1. Is it really true that judgmental people do the very things they judge others for?


2. How is it that we can be so blind?


3. What can we do to get the blinders off?

# 5. The Fishing Pond

*Or do you think lightly of the riches of his kindness and forbearance and patience, not knowing that the kindness of God leads you to repentance? But because of your stubbornness and unrepentant heart you are storing up wrath for yourself in the day of wrath and revelation of the righteous judgment of God.* — Romans 2:4-5

Sin is essentially humankind's attempt to shortcut its way to happiness without God. When, in the short run, it seems to be succeeding, the temptation is to try ever more emboldened ventures into the forbidden. Pride feeds on one's seeming ability to "break the rules" and get away with it.

But it is God's kindness and patience, not cleverness, that allows the wicked to get ahead for a season. He is giving them time to repent. His grace is not inexhaustible, however, if they will not turn from their sins. There comes a day of reckoning for those who continuously flaunt his laws.

There is another side to this equation. It is easy for those who walk the "straight and narrow" to become jealous of the rulebreakers and resentful of the rules.

"Joe got a promotion at work because he padded his figures, while the boss came down on me because my honest figures weren't as good as Joe's."

The heavy temptation is to do something to "even up the odds." Psalm 73 speaks to that issue.

In the long run, sin will always catch up with the sinner, and righteousness will be rewarded. For those of us wishing to live God's way, it really comes down to a matter of faith.

---

**Characters:** use teenagers for this sketch
Buford
Millicent
One hidden person

**Setting:**
Have a *No Trespassing* sign about ten feet from the stage left exit. A barrier is erected below this area to hide the person and things in the fishing pond.

(*Enter Buford from stage right. He is carrying his fishing pole, a tackle box, and a lawn chair. He walks right by the sign, sits down, and casts his line into the "pond." His pole consists of a wooden stick, string, and a clothespin at the end acting as a hook. Millicent now enters from stage right carrying the same items, but stays on the good side and casts her pole into the pond which also has a barrier erected but nothing behind it. After a few seconds Buford gets his first catch — a twenty dollar bill*)

**Buford:** Excellent! I can always use more of you. (*Removes it from the clothespin, kisses it, and puts it in his tackle box. Millicent notices, but says nothing and just keeps fishing. Buford casts his line in again and quickly pulls up a small hand mirror. He removes it from the "hook" and admires* *himself. Millicent takes more interest*) Outstanding! I am totally the bomb! Hey, Millicent, you'd do a lot better over here.

**Millicent:** The sign there says, "No Trespassing," Buford.

**Buford:** (*Looks at it and answers flippantly*) So it does.

**Millicent:** I've heard that the owner will prosecute anyone who violates his property. If I were you, I'd get away from there.

**Buford:** (*Casts his line back into the pond*) You ain't me. Besides — I've been fishing here for years. Caught lots of good stuff. Never seen any owner. Don't think he even exists. (*The line tugs*) Here comes another catch! (*Battles hard on this one and finally pulls up the cover of some magazine with the worldly picture of a young woman on it. Use discretion here*) Oh, you sweet thing! I am in love! (*Hugs the picture*) You ain't gonna catch nothing over there. This is where the killings are made.

(*Millicent gets up and carries her things over to the sign, but not across it. She hesitates*)

**Millicent:** There's a reason for this sign.

**Buford:** It's to ruin our happiness. (*Takes the sign down*) Come on, Millicent. Live a little.

(*Millicent is sorely tempted, but finally becomes resolute*)

**Millicent:** No. I think I'll stay on this side. You do what you want, but I don't care to run afoul of the owner.

(*Buford bursts into a mocking laughter as Millicent goes back to her pond and casts in*)

**Buford:** You really believe in all that nonsense? Guess some people just don't have any brains.

(*Millicent looks at Buford briefly. His comment has hurt. But she answers nothing and continues to fish. After a few more seconds, each gets up and exits to his or her nearer side*)

## Discussion Questions:

1. Have you ever felt resentful of someone who has gotten ahead of you through cheating?

2. Is "everybody else is doing it" a good reason to do it?

3. What are some of the negative consequences, both immediate and future, for those who leave the "straight and narrow"?

4. What are the rewards for staying on the right path?

# 6. The Room Of Death

*For all have sinned and fall short of the glory of God, being justified as a gift by His grace through the redemption which is in Christ Jesus....* — Romans 3:23-34

The word "gospel" means "good news." But in order to understand the good news, we must first realize the bad news. "All have sinned and fall short of the glory of God." But it is that stubborn sin nature, in its various forms, that gets in the way and enables the god of this world to blind "the minds of the unbelieving, that they might not see the light of the gospel of the glory of Christ" (2 Corinthians 4:4).

The following sketch shows six people in a room (this world) of condemnation and death. The first five exhibit five common negative responses to God's laws (the scroll). The sixth is fertile soil that hears the gospel and responds positively.

---

**Characters:**
Six persons (either sex)
　Irreverence
　Pride
　Legalism
　Hatred
　Licentiousness
　Unworthiness
Decreer
Substitute

**Setting:**
The stage is dark and empty except for a closed door standing broadside to the audience.

(*Lights come on. The Six enter from stage left with the Decreer following behind them*)

**Irreverence:** This is an outrage! Nobody has a right to herd me anywhere. Somebody's going to pay for this.

**Pride:** (*To the Decreer*) Who do you think you're pushing around? I'm an important person.

**Decreer:** (*Stands by the door and unrolls a scroll*) Hear ye! Hear ye! Hear ye all! The king has declared this to be the room of condemnation and death. The door you see is the only way out. Only those who satisfy the demands on this scroll are permitted to exit. (*Tapes the scroll to the doorway. He exits through the door and closes it behind him*)

**Unworthiness:** What does it say?

**Legalism:** "You shall have no other gods before me. You shall not make for yourself an idol. You shall not take the name of the Lord your God in vain. Remember ..."

**Irreverence:** Well, whoop-de-do. Come on. Let's blow this place. (*Goes over and attempts to open the door. It won't open*)

**Pride:** (*Laughs at Irreverence's failure*) What we need here is a Harry Houdini. That's me. (*Does a "sleight-of-hand" and produces a key which he holds up for everyone to see. Then he takes a bow and confidently strides over and inserts the key. The door won't open*)

**Legalism:** You people are going about this all wrong. You do what the scroll says. Then you just open it and walk through. (*Runs his finger rapidly down the scroll, snaps his finger as if to say "It's a snap," and pulls easily at the door. It won't open. He tries harder. It still won't open*)

**Hatred:** Anyone that would trap us like this is cruel and unworthy of us. I hate him! And I hate these laws! (*Rips the scroll off the door, tears it in two, and tosses it to the ground. He bangs on the door*) I demand immediate release!

**Licentiousness:** Ain't no way, pal. And since we're all going to die here anyway, let's party while we can. (*Does not go near the door*)

**Unworthiness:** I've broken all these laws many times. (*Picks up the torn scroll, fits it together as best he can, and looks at it mournfully*)

(*Suddenly, the door opens from the other side. In walks the Substitute, dressed in a white robe. He looks like Jesus. He closes the door behind him, takes the torn scroll from Unworthiness, and then stands directly in front of the door*)

**Substitute:** I have come to set you free from the condemnation of this scroll. You may all leave through this door after shaking my hand.

**Irreverence:** What makes you so special? (*With that he walks away from the Substitute and the door to an extreme corner of the stage*)

**Pride:** I only shake hands with people worthy of *me*. (*Walks to another extreme corner of the stage*)

**Legalism:** I don't need you. Give me the scroll and let me do this myself. (*Holds out his hand for the scroll. The Substitute reluctantly hands it back to him*)

**Substitute:** You cannot do these perfectly. You need me.

**Legalism:** I can do them better than anyone else. That should be more than enough. (*Walks just a few feet from the door and stands holding the scroll and facing the audience*)

**Hatred:** So you're the one who trapped us here. Shake your hand? If I had a gun, I'd shoot you! (*Finds another extreme corner of the stage and turns his back on the Substitute*)

**Licentiousness:** How's the party life on the other side?

**Substitute:** I offer a life of purpose.

**Licentiousness:** No thanks, then. I like it better here. (*Stays where he is, but also turns his back on the Substitute. He gets out a little ball, tosses it a few feet in the air and catches it three times*)

**Unworthiness:** (*Walks up hesitantly to the Substitute*) I am unworthy of shaking your hand.

**Substitute:** Then I take it gladly.

(*They shake hands. The Substitute opens the door for Unworthiness. Unworthiness is about to go through, but then notices that the Substitute intends to stay in the room*)

**Unworthiness:** Are you not coming also?

**Substitute:** No. I must remain for a time.

**Unworthiness:** Why?

**Substitute:** If I do not remain here, you cannot go there. Trust me.

(*Unworthiness gives the Substitute a spontaneous hug which is returned. Then he goes through the door and shuts it behind him. All exit, but no one else through the door*)

## Discussion Questions:

1. What attitudes keep a person from honoring God? What is the thinking behind such attitudes?

2. Have you ever done something sacrificial for another, only to see that same person respond negatively to you? How did it make you feel?

3. How do you think it makes God feel when people reject the sacrifice of his Son for their sins?

4. What kind of spirit does God love? (See Psalms 51:17, 138:6; James 4:6)

# 7. The Club

*Now to the one who works, his wage is not reckoned as a favor, but as what is due. But to the one who does not work, but believes in Him who justifies the ungodly, his faith is reckoned as righteousness.* — Romans 4:4-5

Why doesn't God just take everyone to heaven? Because those who don't want God here, won't want to be with him there. Because unwilling residents of heaven would pollute it, making it no different than what we have on earth. Because God's holy character cannot allow for an unholy presence in his kingdom.

Why doesn't God accept those who sincerely strive to work their way into his kingdom? Romans 4:4 answers that question. If such a thing were possible (and it isn't because "all have sinned and fall short of the glory of God"), persons in that category would have no sense of gratitude to God for his grace, hence no love for God, and no desire to worship him. Heaven would then also be polluted.

For those reasons (and probably many others) God has ordained that only faith in him, and in his work of redemption for us through his Son, is the valid means for entry into his kingdom.

---

**Characters:**
Sergeant at Arms
Outsider (wearing a chest full of medals)
Four varied people

**Setting:**
The doorway of an exclusive club.

(*The Sergeant at Arms stands at the doorway. An Outsider comes up and attempts to gain entry*)

**Sergeant at Arms:** Your entry pass, please.

**Outsider:** Entry pass? I don't have any entry pass. But I'm a great guy. I'm the kind of person you want around here. Stand aside.

**Sergeant at Arms:** Sorry, you must have an entry pass.

**Outsider:** This is ridiculous. How do you get this entry pass?

**Sergeant at Arms:** Glad you asked. The owner's son has already purchased one exclusively with your name on it. You simply go to him, ask, and you shall receive.

**Outsider:** That's all? There has to be a catch to this. Don't I have to pay some membership fee? I've got lots of money. How about some heroic deed? Look at all these medals I've won.

**Sergeant at Arms:** Quite impressive. But this club is open only to those who go to the owner's son.

**Outsider:** But if that's all it takes, there's no challenge — no sense of accomplishment. I won't be able to pat myself on the back and say, "Way to go, stud."

**Sergeant at Arms:** And no sense of need for the owner's son.

(*Four people of varied ages, races, economic stature, and so on appear at the doorway*)

**Sergeant at Arms:** May I see your entry passes, please?

(*Each shows an entry pass and is motioned through the door*)

**Outsider:** You mean anybody can get in here?

**Sergeant at Arms:** No, sir. Only those with an entry pass.

**Outsider:** But if that's all it takes, all kinds of undeserving people will get in.

**Sergeant at Arms:** Starting with yourself, sir.

**Outsider:** Oh, you insult me. Well, if that's how it is, I want nothing to do with this club. (*Turns around and walks away*)

**Sergeant at Arms:** As you wish, sir.

## Discussion Questions:

1. Why doesn't God just take people to heaven when they die?

2. Why does God reject good works as the criterion by which we gain entry into heaven?

3. Why do so many stumble over faith, and instead try to work their way into God's favor?

# 8. The Interview

*Yet, with respect to the promise of God, he did not waver in unbelief, but grew strong in faith, giving glory to God, and being fully assured that what He had promised, He was able also to perform.* — Romans 4:20-21

Why does God put such a premium on faith? Because faith brings glory to him. Faith acknowledges our helplessness and God's faithfulness. Faith sees a way above our human circumstances and gives us hope of a better future. Faith enables us to visualize and then accomplish the impossible with God's wisdom and strength. Faith attracts others to the riches of God's kingdom.

---

**Characters:**
Anchorman — Everett
Yolanda Shickamagua
Faith Michals

**Setting:**
The newsroom of a local television station. The Anchorman and Yolanda must be well dressed. Yolanda needs a microphone to speak into and put to Faith's mouth when she speaks.

**Anchorman:** And finally tonight, the incredible saga of an eight-year-old girl who survived against all odds. Yolanda Shickamagua has an exclusive interview with the survivor, Faith Michals. Yolanda?

**Yolanda:** Thanks, Everett. This is Faith Michals who ought to get into the *Guinness Book of World Records* somewhere in the endurance section. She treaded water on the high seas for fourteen hours before finally being rescued. Faith, tell us what happened.

**Faith:** My dad and I were in our boat going to Catalina Island early in the morning before dawn. I was asleep. Next thing I knew, I was in the water with my dad. He said a big boat had hit us without even knowing it. We didn't even have time to get our life jackets on. We were about three miles from shore, but I couldn't swim that far, and my dad couldn't carry me all that way. So he told me to tread water until he came back.

**Yolanda:** How were you able to hold out for fourteen hours?

**Faith:** My daddy said he was coming back.

**Yolanda:** That's all?

**Faith:** My daddy would never lie to me. So I just waited.

**Yolanda:** Amazing. Faith, you are a special person.

**Faith:** My daddy is a special dad.

**Yolanda:** That will do it for tonight. This is Yolanda Shickamagua saying, "Good night, everyone."

## Discussion Questions:

1. Why does God put such a premium on faith?

2. How does faith help us to endure hardship?

3. What does faith need to have in order to be valid? (Hint: An object worthy of faith. It is not faith that saves us. It is faith in God's only Son, Jesus Christ.)

# 9. The Soccer Team

*And not only this, but we also exult in our tribulations, knowing that tribulation brings about perseverance; and perseverance, proven character; and proven character, hope; and hope does not disappoint, because the love of God has been poured out within our hearts through the Holy Spirit who was given to us.* — Romans 5:3-5

No one enjoys tribulation. Indeed, our present culture has a decided aversion to pain in any form. But following the path of least resistance will make us weak people. How we desperately need men and women of character who will do the hard, right things when life gets tough.

But where do we get such strength? It comes first from the knowledge that we have a God who cares, who gives wisdom, and who provides that strength. We who follow Christ know that better days are ahead — if not in this life, then in the next. Jesus was able to endure the cross because he saw the joy on the other side of it (Hebrews 12:2). It is precisely that hope that sustains us through our tribulations and, along the way, inculcates perseverance and proven character into our lives.

---

**Characters:**
Mom
Bryan — her fourteen-year-old son
Kevin — her six-year-old son
Amy — her three-year-old daughter

**Setting:**
A living room with an arm chair and a lamp.

### Scene 1

(*Mom enters the home from stage right. She has just returned from work and is exhausted. She flops down in a chair to relax. Almost immediately, Kevin enters from stage left, wearing a baseball cap, and a glove with a ball which he is tossing up and catching*)

**Kevin:** Hi, Mom. Let's play ball!

**Mom:** Not now, Kevin. I've got to get dinner going.

**Kevin:** You hardly ever play ball with me.

**Mom:** Tell you what. Tomorrow's Saturday. We'll go down to the school and I'll pitch to you.

**Kevin:** Okay — and you have to chase the ball.

(*Kevin exits to stage right. Amy enters from stage left. She is crying*)

**Mom:** (*Gets up and then stoops down to hug her daughter*) What's the matter, Amy?

**Amy:** Billy pushed me down. (*Shows her mother her elbow*)

**Mom:** Oh, you have an oueee. Are you hurt just a little, or is it real bad?

**Amy:** (*Through the tears*) Real bad.

**Mom:** Okay, Mommy will make it better. (*Retrieves a small first aid kit and cleans and bandages the oueee*) There — all better. (*She hugs Amy*)

(*Enter Bryan from stage right*)

**Mom:** Hi, Bryan. How did it go at school today?

**Bryan:** Terrible! (*Continues on and exits the opposite side*)

**Mom:** Well, I've got to get dinner on.

(*Mom exits stage right. Amy follows her*)

### Scene 2

(*After bedtime. Someone holds an "after bedtime" sign for the audience to see. Mom is sitting in her chair reading the Bible. Enter Bryan from stage left*)

**Bryan:** Mom, can I talk to you?

**Mom:** Sure, Bryan. (*Lays aside the Bible*)

**Bryan:** I'm quitting the soccer team.

**Mom:** Why?

**Bryan:** The coach is a jerk. He makes us run wind sprints whenever we mess up. He's always yelling at us. And besides, I'm not going to be a starter. Why should I go through all that torture when I'm hardly going to play anyway?

**Mom:** Well, Son, quitting is a bad habit to get into.

**Bryan:** Dad quit, and he's doing great.

**Mom:** (*This last statement visibly hurts her, but she manages to reply evenly*) I think he will one day regret his decision.

**Bryan:** Mom, how do you do it? It's been two years since Dad left, and somehow you've held everything together.

**Mom:** Bryan, when I was eight years old, my father and I took our boat to Catalina Island. We got rammed by a bigger boat in the darkness, and I found myself in the ocean with my father, three miles from shore, and without a life jacket. My dad told me to tread water until he came back for me. So I treaded water for fourteen hours until he returned.

**Bryan:** How did you hold out so long?

**Mom:** My dad said he was coming back, and I just hung on to his promise.

**Bryan:** So, I'll play first string if I stay with the soccer team?

**Mom:** That's not part of the promise. Maybe you will, but more importantly, you'll discover that you can handle a lot more than you think you can.

**Bryan:** Good night, Mom. Thanks for not quitting on us.

**Mom:** You're welcome, Bryan. Good night.

(*Bryan exits to stage left. Mom stays in her chair and picks up her Bible. Amy's voice comes from off stage*)

**Amy:** Mommy, I'm scared.

**Mom:** Coming, Amy. (*Lays aside her Bible and exits to stage left*)

## Discussion Questions:

1. What is the quickest way to discern a person's character?

2. Why is it important to learn to endure hardships?

3. What is needed to help us endure hardship?

# 10. The Plague

*Therefore, just as through one man sin entered into the world, and death through sin, and so death spread to all men, because all sinned.* — Romans 5:12

When Adam sinned, the entire creation was brought under the curse of death. Since then, most of our human effort has to be devoted either to overcoming the effects of sin, or trying to forget them. Police, locks, doctors, hospitals, lifeguards, work, hair tint, alcohol, entertainment — the list is virtually endless.

Yet when all is said and done, the entire effort cannot alter the inevitable. We still die. Admittedly, this is not a pleasant subject. But the fact of it points clearly to our need for God. We cannot save ourselves.

The following sketch illustrates the hopelessness of humankind without God. And it shows the extent of humankind's answer to its basic problem.

---

**Characters:**
Doctor
Nurse
Hospital patient

**Setting:**
A patient's hospital room.


**Doctor:** Looks like we've lost another one. (*Pulls the sheet up over the patient's head*)

**Nurse:** What's the use? Everybody dies. Why do we all have to suffer just because one foolish man brought the plague to this island?

**Doctor:** We don't need a why. We need an antidote.

**Nurse:** No one has ever come close to finding one.

**Doctor:** We're making progress. Some are living longer.

**Nurse:** And now we're talking about killing them sooner because it's too expensive to keep them longer.

**Doctor:** Why are you bombarding me with all these unpleasant thoughts?

**Nurse:** Because I can't handle them by myself.

**Doctor:** Want to go play tennis? (*Picks up two rackets*)

**Nurse:** I'm right behind you. (*Takes one of the rackets and they exit together*)

## Discussion Questions:

1. What has occupied most of our human effort since Adam sinned and brought death into the world?

2. What are some of the ways those without hope try to deal with death?

3. Supposing man were to somehow discover "the fountain of youth" and abolish death. Would that solve our problems?

# 11. Whose Slave Are You?

*Do you not know that when you present yourselves to someone as slaves for obedience, you are slaves of the one whom you obey, either of sin resulting in death, or of obedience resulting in righteousness?*
— Romans 6:16

One of the great deceptions we frail humans fall prey to is the illusion of self-determination. We think that our choice is between subservience to a rule-making God or the freedom of making our own rules. In truth, the choice is between a relationship with a loving God who has laws designed to help our lives function their best (and who forgives us when we fail), and addiction to sin which brings about our destruction.

Sin is a cruel taskmaster. Only God can truly free us from it. Jesus said, "My yoke is easy, and my load is light" (Matthew 11:30). In experience, the walk of the Christian in fellowship with God is the only true freedom.

---

**Characters:**
Amy
Susan

**Setting:**
Susan is seated at a table facing the audience. She is the picture of despair.

(*Susan is visibly frightened when she hears Amy's voice. Amy sets a large bag down by the table*)

**Amy:** Hi, Susan. I brought you over a few things you might be needing.

**Susan:** Thanks Amy. You people from the church are the only ones who have shown me any love or understanding for my situation.

**Amy:** Some of us have been there, too. (*Takes a seat beside Susan*)

**Susan:** I don't know what got into my head. I knew it was foolish, but it all seemed so beautiful. How could I have been so stupid?

**Amy:** You weren't stupid, Susan. You were just weak like the rest of us. That's why you need God.

**Susan:** Hold on now, Amy. I don't need any God. (*Stands and comes out from behind the table to animate her words as she recites the poem. The last two lines are delivered triumphantly*)

In the fell clutch of circumstance
I have not winced nor cried aloud.
Under the bludgeonings of chance
My head is bloody, but unbowed.

It matters not how strait the gate,
How charged with punishment the scroll,
I am the master of my fate:
I am the captain of my soul.*

**Amy:** Are you, Susan? Give me a call if you need anything else.

(*Amy exits to stage left. Susan's countenance returns to despair. She exits to stage right*)

*From "Invictus" by William Ernest Henley

## Discussion Questions:

1. How does the rejection of God in order to pursue our own pleasures bring about the experience of bondage?

2. How does submission to the will of God for our lives bring about the experience of freedom?

3. Why do so many choose bondage over freedom?

4. How can we best demonstrate to others the "more excellent way" of following Christ?

# 12. Poison

*For the wages of sin is death.*                           — Romans 6:23

What fools we mortals be. James Bond taught us that with suave dexterity and cleverness we can break all the rules and still stay one step ahead of disaster. Clean needles enable us to shoot heroin safely. Condoms provide us with safe sex. "Just don't get caught" is one of our most prized maxims.

Yet despite all our futile efforts to the contrary, God's truth remains. "The wages of sin is death."

---

**Characters:**
Carl
Dr. Smoot

**Setting:**
Carl is seated at a table with his container on it.

(*Dr. Smoot enters and sits on the other side of the table. He opens a folder he has brought with him*)

**Dr. Smoot:** We've gone over all your tests, Carl. Your whole body is in very poor condition.

**Carl:** (*Takes a chug from a huge container with the word "poison" and a skull and crossbones on it. He continually chugs from it throughout the conversation*) I know. I can't understand why I'm feeling so sick. Help me, Dr. Smoot.

**Dr. Smoot:** What you need is a pain killer. Take two of these every day. (*Hands him a bottle of pills*) And try to keep your mind in a peaceful state.

(*Carl puts two pills in his mouth and then gulps them down with another chug of poison*)

**Carl:** Is there anything else?

**Dr. Smoot:** Yes, one more thing — that container.

**Carl:** (*Indignantly*) Hold on. Now you're getting personal. I'm not giving up my juice for anything. You have no right to tamper with my lifestyle. I was born with a predisposition to this.

**Dr. Smoot:** I wouldn't dream of interfering with what you are. But you need to use a clean container, rather than refilling the old, each time you finish a jug, so you're safe from infection while you drink your poison. There's a government agency in town where you can get them for free. Here's their address.

**Carl:** Thank you, Dr. Smoot. You've really helped me.

**Dr. Smoot:** Helping people is the only reason I'm in this business.

(*They shake hands and Carl exits. Dr. Smoot has the satisfied look of one who has really helped his fellow man. He exits the other way*)

## Discussion Questions:

1. What are some "clean containers" people use to try to beat the consequences of sin?

2. What are some "pain killers" people use?

3. What is the problem with using "clean containers" or "pain killers"?

4. What should be the Christian attitude toward people caught up in addictive lifestyles?

# 13. The New Creation

*Therefore, my brethren, you also were made to die to the Law through the body of Christ, that you might be joined to another, to Him who was raised from the dead, that we might bear fruit for God.*
— Romans 7:4

This sketch is meant to depict the law as holy, but not heartless. The evil one attempts to use the law to accuse us (Revelation 12:10). The law is meant to show us our need for the Savior (Romans 7:7; Galatians 3:24). Therefore, the law is to be loved and revered (Psalm 119:97).

The law shows the holiness of God. The Savior shows the love of God. Both aspects come together to full satisfaction through Christ's atoning death on the cross (Romans 3:26).

The sketch shows the accused (the girl) caught in a real transgression — and condemned. But she is redeemed through the body of Christ, set free to be joined to him, and made into a new creation. The final part is meant to depict what Luke 15:7 might look like in heaven when one sinner repents.

---

**Characters:**
Scripture Reader
The King
The Page — male or female
The Accuser — male or female
The Girl — eight years old
The Advocate
Honor Guard — six or eight children, male or female

**Special challenge for a motivated director:**
Have the actors do the entire script with English accents. You can greatly adorn this sketch with kingly costumes and choreography. Repeat some of the music passages if you need more time for some fancy choreography. If you have any trumpets or other brass and percussion available, you might get them in on the act. You might even want to hear how measure 32 to the end sounds with church bells ringing above the music. Do it up in grand style. (Piano/organ accompaniment on page 112.)

**Setting:**
Podium at left center front. Throne at center stage.

(*The Scripture Reader walks to the podium with a large church Bible and opens it to Romans 7:4 which he or she reads in the King James Version*)

**Scripture Reader:** The congregation will please come to stillness for the reading of the Holy Scriptures.

"Wherefore, my brethren ye also are become dead to the law by the body of Christ; that ye should be married to another, even to Him who is raised from the dead, that we should bring forth fruit unto God.

May God bless the reading of his word. Amen."

*(The Scripture Reader closes the Bible and sits in the first row. The podium is removed. The Honor Guard enters to the intro music [first eight measures played on piano]. The King enters with great pomp as the music is repeated a little slower. He sits on his throne with the Honor Guard evenly spread to his right and his left. The Page enters to address the King)*

**Page:** Your highness, 'tis vain in hiding,
Must bring to thee an evil tiding.
Seems what some might call a spy,
Hath seen a girl to steal a pie.

**King:** Bring her hither,
In a dither.
Fetch me now this girl of shame,
And the spy that maketh blame.

*(The Page heads to stage left entrance and calls the Accuser forth)*

**Page:** The king doth bid thee now to enter,
Bring the girl here, front and center.

*(In enters the Accuser, dragging the Girl behind. She has pie all over her face. She is flung before the King)*

**Accuser:** This be her that thought was sly,
'Tis the girl that stole the pie.
Caught her munchin' on those cherries,
Such a wench you must bewaries.

**King:** Speak thou, girl, hold nothing back,
Didst thou steal a pie for snack?

**Girl:** Alas, 'tis true, I must admit,
Saw it on a sill to sit,
And it smelled such blissful scent,
That I took, but now repent!
*(Begins to cry)*

**Accuser:** The law is clear, cannot relent,
E'en if one doth now repent.
Such a one can n'er be free,
She must be hanged upon a tree.

**King:** Yes, 'tis true, I am afraid,
'Tis the law, that's how it's made.
I've no choice, but banish thee,
To the place of misery.

**Girl:** I stand condemned for my transgression,
'Tis just and right, I have no question.
But such a lot is dread so great,
Is no way found to shun such fate?

**Accuser:** None at all, my little waif,
To break the law is quite unsafe.
Cast her forth then. Do the deed.
Rid the world of this foul weed!

(*Two of the Honor Guards take the Girl and sadly lead her toward the exit. All are sad accept the Accuser. She is almost gone when the Page utters the next line*)

**Page:** Yet wait, dear sire, behind me see,
Yon cometh One canst set her free!

(*Enter the Advocate*)

**Advocate:** Condemn her not, she is but weak,
Let me for this girl to speak.
I'll give her life that she might see,
All that she was made to be.

**Accuser:** The law saith death to those who break it,
All to me, since none can make it.
'Tis too late, I may be bold,
She to me her soul hath sold.

**Advocate:** 'Tis not so, my wicked crone,
Dost thou accuse before the throne?
'Tis the law she hath transgressed,
And this law, I have addressed.

True indeed, the law saith death,
From such who err, their mortal breath.
But I, for her the price hath paid,
I hung upon a tree and prayed.

Then died, did I upon that tree,
But in my death, didst set her free.
And then was placed within a tomb,
But rose again to seal your doom.

*(The King beckons to the Girl to come to him. She comes trembling. When she arrives, he gently speaks the following words to her)*

**King:** That he did, but thou must see,
Dost thou accept his death for thee?

**Girl:** Yea for mercy, yea for grace,
Yea for life, I thee embrace!

*(She runs into the arms of the Advocate. The Advocate wipes her face clean with a moist towel)*

**Accuser:** Foul, I cry! 'Tis justice missed.
Condemn her now, I do insist!

**King:** On him her sin hath now been placed,
What was hers is now erased!
So get thee hence thou wicked spy,
To the place where thou wilt fry!

*(The Accuser is escorted off quickly by the same two Honor Guards who were escorting the Girl. The King rises and beckons to the audience)*

**King:** Come now for the celebration,
For we have a new creation!

*(The celebration music begins to play on the organ at measure nine. Two Honor Guards place a robe around the Girl at measure seventeen. Two more place a ring on her finger at the repeat of measure seventeen. Two more place sandals on her feet at measure 25. Present these gifts with flair and style. The Honor Guards take up positions across from each other down the center aisle. The King takes a position at the front row of the center aisle. The Advocate takes the Girl by the hand, and the final grand recessional begins at measure 32. Behind the Advocate and the Girl is the Page. Behind the Page is the Scripture Reader. All exit down the center aisle. When the music is finished, church bells continue to ring for about ten seconds, and then begin to fade out.)*

## Discussion Questions:

1. Whom do the different characters represent?

   | | |
   |---|---|
   | The King | The Law |
   | The Girl | Sinful Man |
   | The Accuser | The Devil |
   | The Advocate | The Lord Jesus Christ |
   | The Page and Honor Guards | The Angels in heaven |

2. Are Christians to love the law of God? Why, or why not?

3. What single act of God both satisfies the holy requirements of the law, and enables him to show mercy on those who have broken his law? (See Romans 3:23-26.)

# 14. The Head Case

*For the good that I wish, I do not do; but I practice the very evil that I do not wish.*
— Romans 7:9

Sin is not freedom from the restraint of rules. Sin brings about bondage to self-destructive behavior. Our governmental agencies spend billions trying to educate us about the harmful effects of cigarettes, alcohol, and drugs (why not gambling too?). Yet we smoke and booze and drug ourselves more and more. Nearly everyone recognizes the harmful effects of divorce, but we keep getting divorced. Why?

Because the secular world does not understand its bondage to sin, and to the author of sin (2 Timothy 2:26; 1 John 5:19). No amount of money or human effort can dislodge the world from Satan's grip. Indeed, human effort to do so amounts to trying to extinguish the fire in a blazing home by spraying it with gasoline. The answer is *not* more gasoline.

Jesus came into this world to "save his people from their sins" (Matthew 1:21). Satan's power over us was broken at the cross (Titus 2:14).

But now comes a greater question. Why do Christians struggle so hard with sin if we have been freed from it? Romans 7 speaks of the Christian's struggle. In experience, the Christian, because of the presence of the Holy spirit in his life, is more acutely aware of sin — and of failure. If there truly is freedom in Christ, how do we attain it?

There are formulas derived from Scripture. There are experiences with the Holy Spirit. There are doctrinal fads. For me, I have never found a replacement to spending time in the Scriptures, praying, fellowshiping and serving with other Christians, and telling the lost about Christ. Somehow, if I do my part, God does his. When there is sin, there is confession and repentance.

Freedom in Christ? It is available and experienced. Struggle and failure? It's often there, too. So what else is new? I know the struggle of Romans 7, but also the victory of Romans 8.

The following sketch can be applied either to the lost or to the struggling Christian. The answer is still Christ in either case.

---

**Characters:**
Hank — a man addicted to sin
Logic
Store clerk

**Setting:**
The Store Clerk is in the middle, rear of the stage, behind a counter as a silent observer until his time comes at the end.

(*Enter Hank from stage right, beating his head with an inflatable club. He continues beating his head throughout this sketch. Enter Logic from stage left*)

**Logic:** Why are you doing that?

**Hank:** Doing what?

**Logic:** Beating your head with a club.

**Hank:** I don't know.

**Logic:** What you are doing is not logical. Stop.

**Hank:** I can't stop.

**Logic:** Why not?

**Hank:** I don't know. I just can't.

**Logic:** Let me educate you about the harmful effects of head-hitting addiction. According to a ten-year federally funded study by the National Head-Beating Institute, persons who regularly beat their heads are 87 percent more likely to have headaches, and 36 percent more likely to develop head injuries.

**Hank:** I know it's harmful.

**Logic:** So why don't you stop?

**Hank:** Can't live without it.

**Logic:** Tell you what. Give me the club. I'll dispose of it for you, and then you won't have any more problems.

**Hank:** Hey, I don't know.

**Logic:** If you don't have the club, you won't be able to pound your head.

**Hank:** True.

**Logic:** Well, then. Give me the club.

(*He comes up to Hank who seems very reluctant to give up the club. Finally, Hank beats himself twice more and surrenders it*)

**Logic:** There now. You're cured. Soon, your head will feel a whole lot better.

(*Exit Logic to stage left. Hank becomes increasingly agitated. He doesn't know what to do with his hands. He sees the Clerk put another inflatable club up on the counter. Hank tries to use willpower to stay away from it, but is drawn toward it like a magnet. Finally, he gets to the counter*)

**Hank:** How much for that club?

**Clerk:** One hundred dollars.

**Hank:** One hundred dollars? That's a rip-off!

**Clerk:** I'm betting you want it so badly, you'll pay it.

(*Hank tries to pull away, but can't. Finally, he takes a hundred dollar bill from his pocket, lays it on the counter, and grabs the club. Immediately, he begins to beat his head as he exits to stage right*)

## Discussion Questions:

1. If it is illogical to engage in self-destructive behavior, (e.g., smoking, drugs, daredevil stunts, suicide) why do people do it?

2. Why can't people just stop when they realize they are hurting themselves?

3. If Christians have been set "free from the law of sin and of death," why do we sometimes sin anyway?

4. How can we personally experience victory over self-destructive behavior?

5. How can we help others get free of self-destructive behavior?

# 15. The Dam

*For the law of the Spirit of life in Christ Jesus has set you free from the law of sin and of death. For what the Law could not do, weak as it was through the flesh, God did: sending His own Son in the likeness of sinful flesh and as an offering for sin, He condemned sin in the flesh.* — Romans 8:2-3

This illustration concerns the Christian trying to live the Christian life in the power of the flesh, and how Christ gives us the victory. Christ's redemption on the cross not only saved us from the eternal condemnation of sin, it delivered us from the power of sin in our daily lives. And in its place the Holy Spirit has provided us with a spirit of victory manifested by the fruits of the Spirit in Galatians 5:22-23.

---

**Characters:**
Director
Workers — 1 speaking part
Out-of-towner

**Setting:**
Have a wall built up halfway between center stage and stage right. More materials to build it higher are visible on the wider side of the stage. At extreme stage right is a box with two levers that serve as switches. At the rear of the stage, connected to the end of the wall, is a closed door.

(*Workers enter from stage left in a high state of stress*)

**Director:** Hurry over here, men. The water's beginning to overflow.

(*Several men rush over and stack the wall higher in an attempt to stem the overflow*)

**Director:** Now it's coming in here. Hurry, hurry — we've got a city to protect.

(*The men rush to the new breech. The Out-of-towner enters and watches*)

**Out-of-towner:** What's the trouble here, sir?

**Director:** The dam keeps breaking down. It's all we can do to plug the holes and keep building it higher. Even still, much water escapes to damage our city. Over there, men! Get on it!

**Out-of-towner:** This has got to be wearying.

**Director:** Tell me about it.

**Out-of-towner:** Has it always been this way?

**Director:** When we first came, there was only a trickle of water that caused minor damage to the original structures. Yet it was a nuisance, so we built a small barrier and thought that would solve the problem. But the water kept building up, and soon we had to build a bigger dam. Now the pressure is so great that if the dam burst we'd have a catastrophe. So we have no choice but to keep shoring it up and building it bigger.

**Out-of-towner:** Is this any way to live?

**Director:** Do you have a better idea?

**Out-of-towner:** What if I went over to the other side and shut off the flow of additional water into the lake?

**Director:** You can't get over there. We've tried it. The door is locked.

**Out-of-towner:** But I have the key. (*Produces a key from his pocket and opens the door which he then shuts behind him. He goes over and throws a switch*) Now, what if I then diverted the water in the lake to another channel heading out into the sea? (*Throws another switch*) I think you'll soon begin to notice a difference.

**Worker:** Sir, the water is beginning to recede and the leaks have slowed to a trickle. Can we go home and get some rest?

(*The Director looks at the Out-of-towner*)

**Out-of-towner:** You can all go home and rest. And after a few days you can redirect your energies into beautifying your city.

**Director:** How can we thank you enough?

**Out-of-towner:** You can't. But it is my joy.

(*Exit all*)

## Discussion Questions:

1. Have you experienced the weariness that comes from trying to live the Christian life in the power of the flesh?

2. Why is willpower alone insufficient to keep the laws of God?

3. How do we learn to live under the control of the Holy Spirit?

4. Have you experienced victory over sin in an area of your life through plugging into "the law of the spirit of life in Christ Jesus"?

# 16. A Little Pain

*For I consider that the sufferings of this present time are not worthy to be compared with the glory that is to be revealed to us.*                                  — Romans 8:18

Pain hurts; and suffering is something we'd rather do without. But suffering plays an important role as a cleansing agent in the Christian life (1 Peter 4:1). It causes us to cry out to God for comfort and strength (Psalm 50:15). Having received God's comfort and strength, we are then equipped to minister the same to others who suffer (2 Corinthians 2:4). Finally, it provides a contrast. Food tastes best when we are hungry. Sleep is most pleasant when we are exhausted. Relief is most appreciated when we have been in pain.

The harder life has been for us on earth, the more we will enjoy heaven in the eternal presence of our God. How good will heaven be? The above verse tells us that our present sufferings are not worthy to be compared with it. We will quickly forget the pain of earthly existence like a woman forgets the pain of childbirth after her child is born (John 16:21).

---

**Characters:**
Dad
Amy — his daughter (perhaps eight years old)
Doctor

**Setting:**
The doctor's office. Have a barrier set up on center stage so as to hide the actual injection from view.

**Amy:** Why do I have to get a shot?

**Dad:** To keep you from getting terrible diseases like scurvy, or appendicitis, or Bubonic Plague.

**Amy:** April's parents don't let her get shots, and she doesn't have any diseases.

**Dad:** If they want to take their chances, that's their business. But I'm making sure with you.

**Amy:** Can't the doctor just give me a pill?

**Dad:** It isn't that bad, Amy. Come on now. Be a big girl.

(*The Doctor appears from behind the barrier*)

**Doctor:** All right, young lady. Time to do it. If you're real good, I'll give you a sucker when it's over.

**Amy:** I don't want a sucker.

**Doctor:** Come on. (*They go behind the barrier*)

**Dad:** I'll wait for you on the other side, honey.

(*Amy screams and yells. She finally emerges from the barrier holding a large piece of gauze on her arm. She looks like she's about to die*)

**Amy:** Take me home, Daddy. I can't go to school today.

**Dad:** Oh, now, that's a shame. I wasn't going to take you to school. I was going to take you to Disneyland instead.

**Amy:** Disneyland?

**Dad:** That's all right, Amy. You're too sick to go.

**Amy:** But I'm feeling better now.

**Dad:** No. You need to be in bed. If I took you now in the shape you're in, you might suffer post-traumatic relapse syndrome.

**Amy:** No, I won't! Look! (*Tosses the gauze in a wastebasket and begins to rapidly twirl the needled arm*) I'm completely better.

**Dad:** Well (*Long pause*) ... All right.

**Amy:** Goody! (*Jumps up and down in ecstasy, grabs her daddy's arm, and begins to pull him offstage*) Hurry up, slowpoke!

## Discussion Questions:

1. Do you physically feel better on Monday mornings or Saturday mornings?

2. Have you ever dreaded an impending painful experience? Was the actual experience as bad as you anticipated?

3. Have you ever found yourself wondering where the pain went when you are doing something highly desirable after having done something highly undesirable?

4. Write a paper titled "My First Hour in Heaven." Describe what you see, feel, hear, smell, and touch. You might wish to include a description of seeing Jesus in all his glory, reunions with departed loved ones, or meetings with the saints of old. Describe the feeling in your soul. Read Revelation 4 and 19:1-9, 21, and 22 to help you get started. Share your paper with the group next week.

# 17. The Prom

*And we know that God causes all things to work together for good to those who love God, to those who are called according to His purpose.* — Romans 8:28

Trials take different forms for each of us. For some, it is the loss of health. For others, it might be the heartache of divorce, a financial setback, or the disappointment of not making the team or getting the part.

But the Christian has the above promise from the word of God. Disappointment helps us to grow in Christlikeness, and sometimes turns into better opportunity elsewhere.

It is really a matter of faith. Do we believe God's promise? If we do, the hope that results gives us the strength to persevere until better days.

---

**Characters:**
Bradley — a teenager (about seventeen years old)
June — Bradley's mom
Zelda — a teenager (same age as Bradley)
Agnes — Zelda's mom

**Setting:**
The kitchen table of Bradley's home is on one side of the stage, and the kitchen table of Zelda's home is on the other side. Each mom is busy preparing a meal.

(*Bradley enters his kitchen looking like warmed-over death. He slumps down at the table*)

**June:** (*Her back is turned. She hasn't seen Bradley yet*) Hi, Bradley, How was school today? (*No answer. She turns around and sees him*) My, my. Looks like you've had a rough day.

**Bradley:** I don't want to talk about it.

**June:** Okay. (*Turns back around and goes about her business*)

**Bradley:** I've decided not to go to the prom.

**June:** How come?

**Bradley:** Victoria's going with Edgar. Edgar! What does she see in him?

**June:** Why don't you go with someone else?

**Bradley:** I didn't really want to go anyway.

**June:** That's a shame. Zelda Smith's not going either. I talked to her mother earlier today.

**Bradley:** Zelda? I thought she was going with William.

**June:** They just broke up. No one asked her because they all assumed William was taking her.

**Bradley:** Oh, Mom — Zelda's the ultimate babe.

**June:** So why don't you ask her?

**Bradley:** She's not my type. (*He means, "She'd never go out with me."*)

(*Bradley's side goes quiet. Zelda enters the kitchen on her side*)

**Agnes:** Good morning, Zelda.

**Zelda:** I don't want to talk about it.

**Agnes:** Okay. (*Goes about her business*)

**Zelda:** How could William be so horrid? He waited till the last minute. Then he asked Priscilla to the prom. Why does there have to be so much pain and suffering in the world?

**Agnes:** Well, Zelda, sometimes disappointments lead to better opportunities. Bradley Schmudkins doesn't have a prom date yet.

**Zelda:** (*Suddenly brightening in anticipation*) Bradley? How do you know?

**Agnes:** I talked with his mom earlier today.

**Zelda:** He's a complete stud.

**Agnes:** So why don't you go with him?

**Zelda:** He's not right for me. (*She means, "He'd never ask me."*)

**Agnes:** All right. But I need you to take this recipe over to his mother for me. She really wants it.

**Zelda:** You wouldn't be trying to scheme something now, would you?

**Agnes:** I learned a long time ago never to intervene in things like this. (*Hands Zelda the envelope*) But I really would appreciate you doing this for me.

**Zelda:** All right.

(*Zelda gets up and walks to Bradley's side where she stands nervously at the door. She starts to ring an imaginary doorbell but stops to get out her make-up kit. She gets as pretty as possible. Finally, she gets up the nerve and rings the doorbell. June exits at the doorbell. Bradley gets up and answers the door*)

**Bradley:** Oh, hi, Zelda. (*Pleasantly surprised, but tries to hide it*)

**Zelda:** Hi, Bradley. My mom asked me to bring this recipe over for your mom. I think it's for some kind of broccoli dish. Do you like broccoli?

**Bradley:** It's all right. How are things going?

**Zelda:** Oh, fine. How's it going with you?

**Bradley:** Fine.

**Zelda:** Are you looking forward to the prom?

**Bradley:** I decided not to go. Proms are overrated. How about you?

**Zelda:** I don't do proms either.

**Bradley:** Yeah, we've passed that stage in life.

**Zelda:** It's time to move on to other things. But I might still go if it was with the right kind of guy.

**Bradley:** What kind of guys do you like?

**Zelda:** Just someone who's honest. I hate it when guys put on a front. That's what I like about you, Bradley. You're real.

**Bradley:** Yeah — I try to be honest. And I've always admired that trait in you, too. (*Fidgets about. He wants to ask her to the prom, but can't get up the nerve*)

**Zelda:** Well, guess I gotta go home and feed the dog. It was nice talking to you, Bradley. (*Puts her hand on one of his shoulders and turns to leave. She gets about three steps away*)

**Bradley:** Zelda?

**Zelda:** Yes? (*Doesn't do well in disguising her hopeful anticipation*)

**Bradley:** Do you think maybe you might sorta want to possibly ... (*Can't get it out*)

**Zelda:** Go to the prom with you?

**Bradley:** Yeah.

**Zelda:** Oh, Bradley, I'd love to.

**Bradley:** You would? I mean — good. I'll get the tickets on Monday.

**Zelda:** And I'll find a gown you'll really like. See you, Bradley.

**Bradley:** 'Bye, Zelda.

(*Bradley shuts the door, steps aside to an imaginary window, and moves the curtain to watch her leave. He catches her waving her arms in ecstasy. June enters from behind*)

**Bradley:** Yes!!! (*Raises his arms triumphantly as he turns around, and then sees his mother. He is startled but recovers quickly*) Oh, man. I've just got to do something about this kink in my back.

(*His uplifted arms suddenly change to movements coordinated with his bending and stretching to attempt to pop his back. He exits. June exits a few seconds later. He hasn't fooled her*)

## Discussion Questions:

1. Have you ever experienced a deep disappointment that led you to something far better?

2. Even if your circumstances don't seem to have improved, have you discovered other positive developments from your disappointments?

3. Have you ever been tempted to "rectify" a disappointing situation through carnal methods? What are the problems with such attempts?

4. Does "All things work together for good to those who love God" *guarantee* better circumstances in this life?

# 18. The Marionette

*On the contrary, who are you, O man, who answers back to God? The thing molded will not say to the molder, "Why did you make me like this," will it?* — Romans 9:20

The most absurd presumption of the human race is that we know better than God how we should function, and how we ought to have been made. The human cloning experimentation spawns ultimately from our attempts to "correct" those "mistakes."

This next sketch gives us an idea of how such an attitude might appear to our Maker.

---

**Characters:**
The Puppet Maker
Brianna — a marionette (a girl about ten years old)

**Setting:**
The Puppet Maker's shop.

Piano accompaniment on page 115.

(*The Puppet Maker is putting the finishing touches on his latest masterpiece [the girl]. She is standing rigidly still with her right arm raised and her hand cupped in a "giving an oath" position, and her left arm down to her side with her hand cupped. She is brightly dressed and perhaps even wears a "Raggedy Ann" wig. He rosies up her cheeks and pronounces his masterpiece finished. He is delighted*)

**Puppet Maker:** There now. You're all finished. And what a beautiful thing you are. I will call you Brianna. Let's see how you move.

(*He stands behind her and raises his arms. In each hand is a cross-shaped item that puppeteers use to maneuver their puppets with strings. The audience will have to imagine the strings. He maneuvers his arms and hands above her and she responds with puppet-like movements of her arms, legs, and head. This will take some practice. The Puppet Maker is delighted at the performance of his masterpiece. After about thirty seconds, Brianna suddenly turns around and begins to speak. Until the final dance of this sketch, she continues to make puppet-like movements, but without any direction from her maker*)

**Brianna:** Why does my life have to come with so many strings attached?

**Puppet Maker:** (*Shocked*) You can talk!

**Brianna:** Yes, and I don't appreciate what you've done to me. If I were you, I'd have done a much better job making me.

**Puppet Maker:** I'm not used to my marionettes talking to me like this, Brianna.

**Brianna:** Well, get used to it. And my name isn't Brianna. It's Daffo. (*Picks up a scissors and cuts her strings. Then she struts about in puppet-like movements admiring her beauty, her individuality, and her new freedom. Suddenly, she trips and falls. She moans in pain*) I broke my arm!

(*The Puppet Maker helps her up and takes her to a chair. He examines her arm*)

**Puppet Maker:** It is broken. But I can fix it in about one minute. (*Retrieves his tools and returns with a large screwdriver, a bag of screws, a hammer, and a saw. He begins to work on the arm*)

**Brianna:** I didn't do so well on my own, did I? (*More statement than question*)

**Puppet Maker:** (*"Screws" a bolt into her arm*) There, now. Try the arm out.

**Brianna:** (*Flexes it this way and that, and smiles. She gives the Puppet Maker a big hug*) Brianna really is a pretty name. May I have it back?

**Puppet Maker:** Of course.

(*Brianna picks up the two marionette crosses and gives them to the Puppet Maker. He smiles, reattaches the strings, and gets behind her. The piano music begins and she dances to it as he directs the strings above her. Yet she dances, not like a puppet, but with fluidity and joy. This symbolizes the sense of freedom that comes from living in submission to God. The final few bars of the music are used for their exit*)

## Discussion Questions:

1. Have you ever despised anything about yourself? (e.g., your appearance, your athletic ability, your personality)

2. Have you ever wanted to blame God for the "mistakes" you might think he made on you?

3. How do you think it appears to God when we decide we know better than him what kind of people we ought to be?

4. What might be the ingredients of developing a healthier self-image? (e.g., thanking God for both your strengths and weaknesses, learning to do one thing very well, disciplining your self-talk)

# 19. Mommy's Birthday

*For I bear them witness that they have a zeal for God, but not in accordance with knowledge.*
— Romans 10:2

Zeal is a good thing. It is contagious and is a desirable component for accomplishing tasks. But zeal without knowledge and direction brings about undesirable results.

---

**Characters:**
Daddy — Clarence
Amy — his daughter
Mommy

**Setting:**
The kitchen.

(*Enter Daddy and Amy*)

**Daddy:** Shhh, Amy. It's Mommy's birthday. I'm going to surprise her with a special birthday cake.

**Amy:** But, Daddy, Mommy says you can't boil water.

**Daddy:** Nothing to a cake, Amy. Let's get out the ingredients. (*Puts the necessary ingredients on the counter while Amy gets out the cookbook and looks for cakes*) We don't need that.

**Amy:** We might forget something without it.

**Daddy:** Okay, Amy. You're right. Tell you what. You're a good reader. Why don't you read the directions and I'll do the work.

**Amy:** Okay. Heat oven to 375 degrees.

**Daddy:** I'll put it up to 500 to save time. Now what?

**Amy:** Separate three eggs.

(*Daddy arranges them in a triangle on a large cutting board*)

**Amy:** Beat the eggs.

(*Daddy hesitates, but breaks each open with his hands and continues to beat on them*)

**Amy:** Pour into a large mixing bowl.

(*Daddy lifts up the cutting board and pours the entire concoction, including shells, into the mixing bowl*)

**Amy:** Add two cups of flour.

(*Daddy is puzzled, but looks around the house. He spies flowers in a vase. He takes them*)

**Daddy:** This is probably about two cups. Does it say to chop them up?

**Amy:** (*Looking at the book*) No.

**Daddy:** Those books aren't very accurate, are they? (*Chops up the flowers and throws them in the mixing bowl*) Now what?

**Amy:** Add one cup of sugar.

**Daddy:** Hand me my coffee cup. (*Amy hands it to him. He grabs a container and fills his coffee cup. He dumps it in the bowl. Amy looks at the container*)

**Amy:** Daddy, this says salt.

**Daddy:** Salt? Well, it looks the same, so it can't taste that much different. What else?

**Amy:** Shortening, baking powder, and two cups of milk.

**Daddy:** We don't have any shortening, but this leftover bacon grease will work. (*Dumps it in*) And we're out of milk. But we do have orange juice. We'll call it orange cake. (*Pours some in*)

**Amy:** Okay. It says stir for 300 revolutions.

**Daddy:** One, two, three, six, sixty, hundred and seventy-five, three hundred. Now put it in the oven?

**Amy:** You have to pour it in a cake pan first.

**Daddy:** We haven't got any big enough for all this. (*Puts it in the oven as it is. While ducked down, he also puts in some dry ice for the smoking effect*) See Amy? There's nothing to it. Maybe I've missed my calling in life.

(*Daddy and Amy turn around and face the back. Someone comes out and holds a sign to the audience that says "Ten minutes later." The sign person exits and Daddy and Amy turn back around*)

**Amy:** Daddy, the oven's smoking!

**Daddy:** Yikes! (*Grabs an aerosol can, opens the oven door, and shoots whatever is in the can into the oven*)

**Amy:** Mommy's coming!

**Daddy:** Quick, Amy! (*Turns the oven off. He is in a panic*) Throw this out on the back porch!

(*Amy runs it out the stage left exit. Mommy enters from extreme stage right and heads for the kitchen. Daddy runs from the kitchen and meets her halfway*)

**Daddy:** Happy Birthday, Honey. Have I got a surprise for you!

**Mommy:** Oh, really? What is it?

**Daddy:** How'd you like to have a special birthday breakfast at Aunt Ethyl's Pancake House? I really want to keep you out of the kitchen this morning.

**Mommy:** Oh, Clarence. You're so thoughtful. I'll go get ready.

(*Mommy exits the way she came. Daddy heads the other way*)

**Daddy:** (*Calling*) Amy.

(*Amy enters from stage left*)

**Daddy:** If you promise not to tell about our disaster, I'll take you with us to breakfast at Aunt Ethyl's.

**Amy:** Oh, goody. I'll never tell, Daddy.

**Daddy:** That's my girl.

(*They exit arm in arm*)

## Discussion Questions:

1. Have you ever attempted something with much zeal and no knowledge. How did it come out?

2. Do you tend to read the directions first, or "cut to the chase" in the interest of saving time?

3. Why is it critical to possess a true knowledge of God?

# 20. The School Play

*I say then, they did not stumble so as to fall, did they? May it never be! But by their transgression salvation has come to the Gentiles, to make them jealous.* — Romans 11:11

One of the errors of God's chosen people was to suppose that they had a monopoly on God. But Jesus said, "Do not suppose that you can say to yourselves, 'We have Abraham for our father'; for I say to you, that God is able from these stones to raise up children to Abraham" (Matthew 3:9).

Their arrogance led to the loss of their privileged position and the making of salvation available to the Gentiles. Why? Because the making available of God's salvation to the Gentiles made them grateful, and the Jews jealous. That kind of jealousy can lead to a humbling and a returning to the fold, which is the ultimate purpose of God's counsel.

The following vignette illustrates how God uses this weakness of human nature to accomplish good.

---

**Characters:**
Eloise
Dudley
Priscilla
Edgar
Kirsten
Mr. Baxter

**Setting:**
A drama classroom at a high school. The students are about to audition for the lead parts in the school play. Mr. Baxter, the drama teacher, has not yet entered the classroom. All the students are messing around except for Kirsten, who is hard at studying her lines.

**Eloise:** Hey, Priscilla, want to hear the latest joke?

**Priscilla:** Whatcha got, Eloise?

**Eloise:** Why did the chick cross the road?

**Priscilla:** To get to the other side?

**Eloise:** No, it was because Jesse Donatelli was over there.

**Priscilla:** (*Sighing*) Jesse Donatelli — wish I could get him to ask me out.

**Edgar:** But you wish even more that you could get me to ask you out.

**Priscilla:** Go study your lines somewhere, Edgar.

**Edgar:** Hey, I'm a senior. I've been in seven plays. You know Mr. Baxter's already got me picked for Prince Thomas. And if you get Julia, you get to kiss me.

**Priscilla:** I would never deserve anything like that. (*Meant as a veiled insult*)

**Dudley:** What's so special about Jesse?

**Eloise:** He isn't at all like either of you. That's a good start. And what makes you think Priscilla's getting Julia? I'm Mr. Baxter's favorite.

(*Enter Mr. Baxter*)

**Mr. Baxter:** All right, Act 2, Scene 3. Prince Thomas and Julia. Who's going first?

**Edgar:** I'm on it for Thom.

**Eloise:** I've got Julia.

(*Both come up front carrying their scripts*)

**Mr. Baxter:** Put your scripts away.

**Edgar:** I don't quite have it memorized yet.

**Eloise:** My drilling partner didn't show up for practice. (*Glares at Edgar*)

**Mr. Baxter:** I specifically said that whoever auditions for the leads has to memorize this scene. Sit down, both of you. Is anybody prepared?

(*Nobody speaks for about five seconds. Finally, Kirsten shyly raises her hand and timidly speaks*)

**Kirsten:** I have Julia memorized.

(*Mr. Baxter beckons her up front. The others laugh at the effrontery of this rookie freshman and make disparaging remarks as she heads up to the front*)

**Mr. Baxter:** Okay, Kirsten. I'll read Prince Thomas for you to play off of. "Julia, fair damsel. Thou seemest of a disquieting temper. Pray tell, what doth ail thee sore?"

**Kirsten:** (*Acting*) "I fret for thy life, my lord. Would that thou couldst take my hand apart from such mortal peril."

**Mr. Baxter:** "Ah, but I would fain be worthy of thy devotion. The bitter cometh before the sweet. Ere I claim thy hand, I must needs slay the dragon of Hucknall."

**Kirsten:** "But if thou wast to be slain, I should be compelled to wed Balbo."

**Mr. Baxter:** "Fret not thyself, my love. The very thought of that knave raiseth in me yet greater resolve. N'er shall he have thee."

**Kirsten:** "Then off, brave prince — to slay the dragon. But take with thee this fairing of my undying love." (*Pretends to shear off a lock of her hair and hands it to him*) A part of me shall be with thee in thine ordeal."

**Mr. Baxter:** Outstanding, Kirsten. You're my Julia!

**Kirsten:** Oh, I can't believe it! Me? (*Gasps delightedly*)

**Mr. Baxter:** I'll be calling Jesse Donatelli about Prince Thomas. He'd be perfect for the part. Well, that's it for today, gang. Tomorrow is the audition for the supporting roles. Be ready with Act 1, Scene 2 — memorized.

(*Exit Mr. Baxter. Kirsten exits the other way, walking about six inches above the floor. She can't believe she actually has the lead. The two girls exit a few seconds later — green with jealousy. Then the two boys exit with Edgar, saying this last line as they head out the door*)

**Edgar:** Do you think maybe I could get Balbo?


## Discussion Questions:

1. Have you ever had someone chosen ahead of you? How did it make you feel? Did it change anything in your life?

2. Why did God allow or cause a partial hardening of Israel? (See Romans 11:25, 31-32.)

3. Why does God shut people up in disobedience in order that he might then show mercy to them?

# 21. The Task

*And do not be conformed to this world, but be transformed by the renewing of your mind, that you may prove what the will of God is, that which is good and acceptable and perfect.*
— Romans 12:2

God's way and man's way are two diametrically opposed thought processes and lifestyles. We serve God based on our gratefulness for his mercy toward us. The world seeks happiness through self-fulfillment, and responds with hatefulness when others block that path.

The world lives for the here and now, with pleasure as its main object. Christians live for the eternal, with purpose transcending pleasure.

The world lives by the pragmatic — whatever works. Christians live by principle, making decisions based on moral absolutes, because we serve a holy God.

The following sketch shows how many of us attempt to mix the two together and live a dual life. Sorry. It's one or the other — but not both.

---

**Characters:**
One actor — no dialogue


This sketch has no dialogue and uses only a single actor.

The task is for the person to lift two fairly large, new U-Haul-type boxes simultaneously and exit with them to stage left. They are packed to weigh about 25 pounds each and are set in the middle of the stage. One has "God's way" imprinted on the side facing the audience. The box next to it has "Man's way" on it. A rectangular table is nearby.

The actor enters from stage right. He (or she) walks up to the boxes, and with great difficulty, lifts one on top of the other. Then he attempts to lift both, but cannot. He steps back to size up the situation. Then he lifts one and uses all his strength to get it on the table. Then he lifts the other to the table (always keeping the labels facing the audience). Now he struggles to finally get one stacked on top of the other. He draws back to rest a few seconds. Then he attempts to lift both from the table. He cannot. He draws back again to rest and think. He goes to the front of the table, stoops, and tries to pull them both on to his back in the stooped position. They won't budge. Now he steps back again frustrated. There has to be a way. He tries lifting both from the table again. As soon as they clear the table, they crash to the floor. He steps back again. Inspiration comes. He runs off to stage right and returns with a very short, light duty hand-truck. He puts one box on it and then the other. The hand-truck can't handle both at once. They won't tilt back together. Finally, they do, but the second is above the top of the hand-truck and slides off sideways. Now he steps back again and thinks a long time. Finally, he lifts the one marked "God's way" and exits to stage left.

**Special challenge for the motivated actor:**
Do this in the Chaplinesque style of an old silent movie with appropriate costuming and piano music to accompany the stage action. You may want to adjust the stage directions to fit the character. Just stay within the parameters. You can't lift both boxes at once and carry them to the exit. Leave your pastor time for the message.


## Discussion Questions:

1. Contrast the values by which the world lives and how a Christian is called to live. (Let the people come up with this list on their own and add to it.)

    | **Worldly Values** | **Christian Values** |
    |---|---|
    | Love yourself first — then others | Love God, first, then others, then yourself |
    | Happiness through self-fulfillment | Joy through knowing God |
    | Living for present world — pleasure | Living for the eternal — purpose |
    | Whatever works — pragmatic | Whatever is right — principle |
    | Emphasis on personal rights | Emphasis on responsibilities |

2. Have you ever faced a dilemma between doing the hard, right thing, or the easy, wrong thing? What did you decide, and how did it come out?

3. What is the best way to ensure that you will do the right thing if and when the next crisis comes? (Hint: Do the little right things every day.)

# 22. The Flower

*For just as we have many members in one body and all the members do not have the same function, so we, who are many, are one body in Christ, and individually members one of another.*
— Romans 12:4-5

The body of Christ is likened here and in chapter 12 of 1 Corinthians to the human body. As the human body consists of many parts, all placed by God for an important purpose, so the body of Christ consists of many parts, some more conspicuous than others, but all essential.

What is the will of God for any of his children? It is simply to walk in fellowship with him and use the gifts he has given us to fulfill our place in the body of Christ. We run into trouble when we try to be something else.

---

**Characters:**
Three flowers — girls between five and nine years old wearing ballerina tutus or bright Easter dresses with flower petals extending from around their heads
One family
    Dad
    Mom
    Billy — son, about eight years old
    Amy — daughter, about six years old
Gardener
Older Couple
    Bessie
    Harold

**Setting:**
A flower garden in a park or public place.

Piano accompaniment on page 115.

*(The three Flowers position themselves halfway between center stage and stage left. They crouch with their feet flat on the floor, their heads down, and their arms folded over their heads. They are flowers folded down for the night. The pianist plays the passage from "The William Tell Overture." As the pianist plays, the two outside Flowers slowly rise, their arms extend out, and their heads come up so that they are looking into the bright sun. Both have big smiles on their faces. They are fully blossomed by the time the pianist stops. At measure six the middle Flower begins to rise and becomes fully blossomed, and smiling, by the end of the William Tell passage. The Family enters from stage right)*

**Mom:** Oh, look, children. Look at the beautiful flowers!

**Amy:** How pretty. (*Goes over and feels the petals on one*)

**Mom:** You and Billy stand behind them. I've just got to get a picture.

**Billy:** Do I have to? I hate flowers. They're ugly.

**Dad:** Do as your mother says, Billy.

**Billy:** (*Unhappily*) All right.

(*Amy and Billy stand behind the Flowers. Amy gives a big smile. Billy manages a faint smile. Mom snaps the picture*)

**Mom:** That's going in our photo album.

**Amy:** Can I take this one home? (*Tugs on the arm of the Flower nearest center stage. The Flowers must stand statue still and be impervious to all of this*)

**Dad:** No, honey. They're here for everyone to enjoy.

**Mom:** Come on, now. We've got to get Amy to her dance lesson.

(*All exit to stage left. When they are gone, the Flowers break their statue poses, except that their feet must stay rooted, and begin to converse with each other*)

**Center Flower:** I don't want to be a flower anymore.

**Left Flower:** What's wrong with being a flower?

**Center Flower:** It's boring.

**Right Flower:** What do you want to be instead?

**Center Flower:** A dancer, like Amy.

(*With that she uproots one leg and then the other, goes over to right, center stage, and begins to dance to the piano music, starting at measure 11. She does elegant leaps and pirouettes like a ballet dancer. The other two Flowers also dance in unison but stay within two feet of their roots. But then the music changes at measure 20 and the uprooted Flower begins to wilt. The dancing of the two slows down as the music slows down. Finally, the uprooted Flower flops down on the floor at measure 24 and all dancing stops*)

**Right Flower:** Oh dear, oh dear. She wilted!

**Left Flower:** We've got to go and help her.

**Right Flower:** How can we? We'll wilt, too.

**Left Flower:** What do we do?

**Right Flower:** Shhh! Here comes the gardener.

(*The two Flowers revert to their bloom poses. Enter gardener from stage right. He is whistling a happy tune*)

**Gardener:** What do we have here? My, my, you poor thing. (*Picks up the "wilted" Flower and puts her in his wheelbarrow. Then he wheels her over to her planting position and places her on it in her original stooped position. Then he packs soil around her. He gets out his green garden pail and pours "water" around her feet. As he pours the water, the pianist repeats measures 1 through 5. She slowly rises and blooms again with a grateful smile on her face*) There now. You stay where you belong. Flowers don't do well out of the soil.

(*Gardener exits to stage left. The Older Couple enters from stage right*)

**Bessie:** Look, Harold! Look at the beautiful flowers!

**Harold:** They sure are pretty, Bessie.

**Bessie:** (*Comes up to the center Flower and smells it*) Magnificent!

**Harold:** Yep. Thank God for flowers. Don't know what we'd do without them.

(*They exit to stage left*)

## Discussion Questions:

1. Brainstorm on the chalkboard. Why do we often try to be something other than what God made us? (Partial list below)
    To impress others
    Copying someone we admire or envy
    Wanting to be cool and fit in
    The grass is always greener on the other side
    Perception that some gifts are better than others

2. How do people trying to be other than what they are look to you?

3. How might we go about finding our particular niche?

4. What characterizes people who have found their place and are faithfully serving in it?

# 23. Getting Even

*Never take your own revenge, beloved, but leave room for the wrath of God, for it is written, "Vengeance is mine, I will repay," says the Lord.*     — Romans 12:19

"Vengeance (ven'jans) noun 1. Eye for eye, tooth for tooth; a fair, satisfying and rapid way to a sightless, toothless world" (Calvin Miller).

The Scriptures make it clear that vengeance is a concept foreign to the Christian life. Part of the faith we have as believers involves the knowledge that revenge against those who hurt is both wrong and unnecessary. God will repay them.

There are a number of reasons God forbids us to take revenge on those who might deserve it. For one, we really don't know who deserves what. God judges perfectly. We humans are quite fallible, especially when it involves injury done to ourselves.

Secondly, revenge can be sweet to the taste, but it will injure our souls. Those who constantly go for the "pay back" become ugly human beings.

Then too, revenge can escalate until both parties to the conflict, and many around them, are deeply wounded. Have you seen any divorces recently?

What is the difference between revenge and punishment? Revenge is retaliation for real or imagined (or exaggerated) harm done to oneself. Punishment is justice meted out by proper authority when appropriate. In society, that may involve law enforcement and the courts, or the schools. In a family, it's a parent disciplining a child. One question you might ask yourself as a parent before disciplining your child is, "Why am I doing this?" Is it punishment administered to correct the child's behavior out of a motivation of love, or is it retaliation because the child hurt you?

What is the Christian alternative to revenge? "If your enemy is hungry, feed him...."

"But he doesn't deserve to be fed," you might protest. That may be true, but who among us deserves God's mercy? Ultimately, we show mercy to others because God was merciful to us. If everyone obeyed God in this regard, the world would both see and chew a lot better.

**Characters:**
Dennis — a boy about twelve years old
Isaac — a boy about twelve years old
Two ladies to hold up the barrier
Dentist
Eye Doctor

**Setting:**
The two boys are seated at a table at center stage getting ready to open their soda cans. Their clothing is dirty and torn. One chair is set at extreme stage left, and one at extreme stage right.

**Dennis:** Boy, there's nothing like a cold soda after a friendly game of tackle football, right, Isaac?

**Isaac:** Yeah, Dennis. And that's what I like about our football games. They're friendly. Nobody gets mad. We just bash each other and have a great time.

(*Isaac opens his soda can near enough to Dennis so that a little of the pressurized spray accidentally hits him. Dennis takes a few seconds to decide how to react. Then he shakes his can so as to increase the spraying pressure and opens it to spray Isaac deliberately. Isaac pauses for a second, then rises to his feet, reaches out, and gives Dennis the slightest shove with one finger. Dennis pauses, and then shoves Isaac back just a little harder with two fingers. Isaac goes for a full hand shove. The two women now come on stage with a barrier that says "censored" on it. Dennis gets in his two-hand retaliation shove just before the barrier goes in front of him and Isaac. Behind the barrier can be heard the sounds of a brawl. The two women just stand there holding up the barrier and smiling at the audience. Finally, the fight ends and Dennis emerges to sit on the stage right chair. His right hand covers his mouth. Isaac goes to the left chair. He is covering one eye. The two ladies exit the opposite direction from which they entered with the barrier. Enter the Dentist from stage right*)

**Dentist:** So, I understand you got in a fight. Open up and let me see. (*Looks in Dennis' mouth for a few seconds*) Looks like you got popped pretty good. Tell you what, Dennis. You're going to need two compost fillings with pin buildups. I think I can fix this, but it's going to take time and involve some discomfort on your part. I really don't recommend fighting as part of any well-rounded program in proper dental care.

**Dennis:** Totally worth it.

**Dentist:** How's that?

**Dennis:** You oughta see what I did to the other guy.

(*Dennis and the Dentist now exit quietly. The Eye Doctor enters on Isaac's side*)

**Eye Doctor:** That's a pretty good shiner there, young man. Get in a fight?

**Isaac:** Yep.

**Eye Doctor:** Well, let me see what we've got. (*Turns on his little flashlight and looks around Isaac's eye*) You have two corneal abrasions and considerable ecchymosis around the eye socket. I'm, going to give you some Polymyxin B ointment and put a patch over it. You can expect impaired vision out of that eye for about a month. You know, Isaac, the eye is a very delicate instrument. It doesn't do well when colliding with a fist. It's biologically incorrect.

**Isaac:** Yeah, well you oughta see the other guy. He won't be eating anything but soup for a while.

(*Isaac and the Eye Doctor exit*)

*Ecchymosis — black eye

## Discussion Questions:

1. What are some reasons why God forbids his people from taking revenge?

2. What is the Christian alternative to revenge?

3. What is the difference between revenge and punishment?

# 24. The Alaskan Cruise

*Render to all what is due them: tax to whom tax is due; custom to whom custom; fear to whom fear; honor to whom honor.* — Romans 13:7

One of the marks of good Christian stewardship is to honestly and faithfully pay our taxes when they are due. Jesus paid taxes (Matthew 17:24-27). Taxes are the legitimate means for civil government to operate and enforce laws, based on God's principles, that facilitate the general welfare of the people under its jurisdiction (Romans 13:3-4).

But what if government becomes oppressive, collecting too much tax, and involving itself in areas outside the biblical framework? I believe that our first course is to pay our taxes anyway, but work within the system to change the laws for the better. All Christians of eligible age should vote. Some should become actively involved in government. If we don't, the government will most certainly become oppressive. Such is the nature of human beings without the Christian influence.

There is a point where we must draw a line and refuse to submit to government. That is when it forbids us to do what God commands, or commands us to do what God forbids. Daniel prayed anyway (Daniel 6:10). The apostles witnessed for Christ anyway (Acts 5:28-29).

If we are going to resist, we must first examine our own motivations. If, as in this next sketch, we rationalize our cheating as protestation against government policy, when our real motivation is to finance that Alaskan cruise, we are on thin ice. It is wise also to bear in mind that if we choose to defy our government, be it for legitimate reasons or not, there will be a price to pay.

---

**Characters:**
Hamilton
Jerusha


**Hamilton:** I don't believe this! Only $517 on our tax refund this year. What happened?

**Jerusha:** Don't you remember, Hamilton dear? We stopped tithing.

**Hamilton:** Well, Jerusha, we had to cut somewhere — inflation.

**Jerusha:** You're right. New cars do cost a lot more than they used to.

**Hamilton:** Thanks to our crazy politicians. But now I ask you, how will we ever pull off our Alaskan cruise on $517?

**Jerusha:** I don't know. Maybe we should just settle for bed and breakfast in Pottawattamee.

**Hamilton:** Come now — we've got to get creative and find another way to reduce our taxes. They waste most of it anyway.

**Jerusha:** That's true enough. Remember the list we got from that Christian family organization? Lots of our tax dollars go to causes we don't believe in.

**Hamilton:** That's it!

**Jerusha:** What's it?

**Hamilton:** We'll just add up all those bogus government expenditures, figure what percentage it is of the total national budget, and deduct that percentage from our tax obligation.

**Jerusha:** But isn't that cheating?

**Hamilton:** Cheating? It's our Christian duty! We'll call it the "Religious Conscience Deduction." Where's that list?

**Jerusha:** Couldn't we wait until this Sunday at least, and hear what our pastor has to say about it?

**Hamilton:** If we do that, we'll never get to Alaska.

(*Hamilton and Jerusha exit*)


## Discussion Questions:

1. Why should Christians honor and submit to civil government?


2. In addition to the above reasons, what else are we obligated to do on behalf of our government leaders? (1 Timothy 2:1-4)


3. What is the first thing we as Christians should do about laws we feel are unjust or unrighteous?


4. At what point are we obligated to resist a law or our government leaders?

# 25. The Donut

*But put on the Lord Jesus Christ, and make no provision for the flesh in regard to its lusts.*
— Romans 13:14

There is an arrogance that sometimes comes with having a little success in life. When things are going well, we may subtly move from praising God to praising ourselves, though we may still be saying all the right words.

With that arrogance comes a carelessness. We suppose we're too strong for "little things" to affect our Christian lives. Carelessness turns to compromise, and compromise to rationalized sin. Sin, like an army, slowly begins to position its soldiers around us under the cover of darkness. When the soldiers are massed, they suddenly attack and overwhelm us before we know now what happened. That is what happened to Samson (Judges 16:18-21).

What will keep a man or woman of God from meeting Samson's fate? Heeding Romans 13:14 is certainly the place to start. But such a stance has no validity without the proper handle of accountability. Do you have a trusted Christian friend to whom you have confided your weaknesses and who is praying for you? Does that friend have your permission to ask you the hard questions at any time? Are you honest with that friend? James 5:16 validates Romans 13:14.

---

**Characters:**
Mr. Higganbotham — Higgy, the president of the corporation
Prudence — well-dressed woman

**Setting:**
The president's office in a large corporation. The office is at stage right. At stage left in "another" room is a table with a single donut on a plate on the table.

*(The president is sitting at his desk as Prudence enters from stage right. The president rises to shake her hand as she reaches him)*

**Prudence:** You sent for me, Mr. Higganbotham?

**Higgy:** Ah, yes. Prudence Famiglietti. I just wanted to commend you for your prodigious sales figures. What's gotten into you?

**Prudence:** I decided to get serious about my life, sir. I went on a diet and lost 22 pounds. That's given me a new confidence. I feel great — like I could conquer the world.

**Higgy:** I admire people with your kind of willpower.

**Prudence:** It's mind over matter. I don't permit even the tiniest exception.

**Higgy:** Well, keep up the good work.

**Prudence:** I intend to, Mr. Higganbotham. Now, I really need to get back to business. What's the shortest way out of here?

**Higgy:** Right through here. (*Points to the stage left exit*) But you might not want to go that way. There's a donut in the next room.

**Prudence:** Come on, now. No little donut's going to derail me. It was good seeing you, Mr. Higganbotham.

**Higgy:** Likewise, Ms. Famiglietti.

(*They shake hands. Prudence opens an imaginary door to the next room. She sees the donut and immediately looks away. She tries to back toward the stage left exit and ends up bumping the table. By now she is shaking with apprehension*)

**Prudence:** Come on, Prudence. Pull yourself together. You can do it. (*Moves two steps toward Higgy's office, tries a wide sweep around the table in the direction of the audience, and then moves toward the exit. She almost makes it. Then abruptly, the trembling stops. She looks at the donut*)

That sure is a nice looking donut. (*Thinks about it a little more*)

You know, a good donut is like a work of art. (*Moves behind the table and admires the work of art*)

Maybe I should smell it. A good art connoisseur uses all her senses. (*Leans down and takes in a good whiff*)

I guess that might also include the sense of taste. (*Takes a tiny nibble. Then she puts it down quickly*)

What have I done? I'd better get out of here! (*Struggles mightily toward the exit. It is as if she is moving against a terrific, invisible force. She stops to catch a breather. More self-talk*)

I took a nibble. Now no one else will want it. The whole donut will be wasted. It's a sin to waste food. (*Goes back, picks up the donut, takes a big bite, and heads off — donut in hand*)

## Discussion Questions:

1. What are some of the greatest temptations we face in this culture.

2. What kinds of attitudes make us more likely to fall when temptation strikes?

3. What are some rationalizations we sometimes use that might lead to giving in to temptation? (Pick a certain temptation such as sexual temptation and have the audience brainstorm.)

4. What are some practical ways to resist temptation? (e.g., avoiding certain places, fleeing, throwing certain items away, asking God for strength, claiming promises, accountability)

# 26. Differences

*Who are you to judge the servant of others? To his own master he stands or falls; and stand he will, for the Lord is able to make him stand. One man regards one day above another, another regards every day alike. Let each man be fully convinced in his own mind.*
— Romans 14:4-5

Of all places, the greatest freedom to be ourselves ought to be found within the body of Christ. God has made us all of different races, economic backgrounds, gifts, preferences, talents, personal viewpoints, and two sexes. With those differences we can each make our own unique contribution to the health of the body.

Cultivation of our differences is not to be confused with tolerance of false doctrine. In the essential doctrines of the Christian faith (e.g., the deity of Christ; the virgin birth; the death, burial, and resurrection of our Lord Jesus Christ; the infallibility of the Scriptures; and so on) there must be unity of belief.

Neither must a cultivation of our differences be used to overlook sin. "He was born that way" or "It's because of her background" might help explain, but will never excuse sin.

But within those parameters let us "celebrate our diversity," learn a little patience with one another, and use our differences to further the kingdom of God.

---

**Characters:** (dressed appropriately for parts)
Youth Pastor
Teenagers in the youth group
    Nerd
    Young Beautiful Thing (YBT)
    Jock
    Rapper
    Cowboy (or Cowgirl)
    Straight-laced, Sober, and Sad (SSS)

**Setting:**
A small room at the church. The Youth Pastor has an easel with paper on it. Before him are six chairs occupied with the other people.

**Youth Pastor:** Pastor Burns (*use your pastor's name*) asked me to plan an outreach program for our community. I need some creative ideas.

**Cowboy:** I gots just the thing. Hows about a rootin' tootin', barn burnin' rodeo, and then a square dance with lotsa fancy pickin' and fiddlin'?

**Jock:** No way. The only cowboys live way out in manure country. What we need here is an evangelistic track meet.

**Nerd:** Brainless, coliseum mentality. A chess tournament would be more intellectually stimulating.

**YBT:** I think we ought to have a Miss (*name of your church*) contest. And just so the others can win something, we'll have first, second, and third runners-up to me.

**Rapper:** Ya got it all wrong. People's in ta movin' anna groovin'.

(*The four who have already spoken move to the rapper's beat according to their characters. The Cowboy starts whirling an lasso over his head. The Jock flexes his biceps on alternating arms. The Nerd snaps his fingers on alternate hands, trying to look cool and looking utterly foolish doing it. The YBT does a cheerleading routine. The SSS stands placidly still*)

**Rapper:** If ya wanna reach da people gotta doa little movin' cuz it's movin' anna groovin' gets da soula a da folka heres a loca so's ya catch 'em wit you fetchin' an ya reach 'em wit ya preachin' an ya gotta do a lotta a da rappin' anna slappin' ...

**SSS:** Apostasy! Apostasy! Jonathan Hamilton Morgan said in 1670, "Cleave ye to the old ways. The tried and true." I won't go past a bean bag toss!

(*The six suddenly get into a horrific, arguing free-for-all. The Youth Pastor stands off to the side in amazement. After about ten seconds he intervenes*)

**Youth Pastor:** Quiet!

(*Everyone abruptly stops*)

**Youth Pastor:** I need to get some further wisdom from Pastor Burns before we go any further on this. We'll get back to this next week.

(*Everyone exits. The six are in three pairs, arguing as they leave*)

## Discussion Questions:

1. In what ways are people different? (e.g., personality, preferences, talents, abilities, background, race, sex, language, economics, convictions, and so on.)

2. Why is it often difficult for people of different backgrounds to work together?

3. What is the great common denominator that ought to enable Christians of different types to work together in harmony?

4. How can we use our differences to further the kingdom of God?

# 27. The Table

*Now may the God who gives perseverance and encouragement grant you to be of the same mind with one another according to Christ Jesus; that will one accord you may with one voice glorify the God and Father of our Lord Jesus Christ.* — Romans 15:5-6

Unity in the body of Christ is a beautiful thing to behold when it works. It is like a symphony orchestra playing many individual parts to produce a beautiful collective sound. Or it might be something as simple as moving a table from one place to another with a minimum of fuss.

---

**Characters:**
Four table movers — males
Leader — male

**Setting:**
A table at center stage.

**Leader:** All right, gentlemen. We need to move this table from here to over there for the ladies' tea this afternoon. Get it done. I'll be back in a minute.

(*Exit Leader. The four gather at the table. The First stands on it and begins to pull the table top up toward him. The Second tries to lift one corner. A Third gets under it and tries to lift it. The Fourth is trying to shove it to where it is supposed to go. The table goes nowhere*)

**First:** What's wrong? Nothing's happening.

**Second:** How can anything happen while you're standing on it? Get off!

**First:** Hey, I'm working the hardest of any of you.

**Third:** This thing's a lot heavier than it looks.

**Fourth:** If you'd get out of my way, I could push it.

**Third:** Oh, so you think I'm in the way. Fine. Do it yourself. (*Starts to walk away*)

**First:** So you're copping out on us?

**Third:** Are you calling me a copper-outer?

**Second:** That's what you're doing, isn't it?

**First:** If we'd all just try a little harder. (*Struggles mightily to pull the tabletop toward himself while he's standing on it*)

**Fourth:** You know, you're a complete moron.

(*The four now go nose to nose in a free-for-all of dispute. The table has gone nowhere. Enter the Leader who watches the free-for-all for a while. Then he blows a whistle*)

**Leader:** Time out! Time out! I see we're having a small problem. Now, would you please take this corner? And you take this corner. That's right. Now you take this corner, and you take that one. Ready? One, two, three, lift. Now move together toward the designated spot. Very good. Thank you. Now the ladies can have their tea. (*Exits*)

**First:** It happened!

(*All are standing around in amazement as if they have just witnessed the parting of the Red Sea. After about ten seconds, they all start slapping each other on the back and doing high fives*)

**Second:** Don't that beat all. (*As a statement*)

**Third:** Wasn't nothin' to it!

**Fourth:** Hey, I take back what I said (*Talking to the First*) about you being a moron. You're really pretty smart.

**First:** You don't do so bad yourself.

**Second:** How about we all go out and celebrate with some ice cold Dr Pepper!

**The Other Three:** Yeah!

(*All exit still slapping each other on the back and doing the high fives*)

## Discussion Questions:

1. Have you ever been part of a team of people that really worked well together in accomplishing tasks? What was that experience like? Have you ever had the opposite experience? What was that like?

2. What are the ingredients that make for good team chemistry?

3. It has been said that a team that works well together is greater than the sum of its individual parts. Is this true? If so, why is it true?

# 28. The Pacesetters

*But I have written very boldly to you on some points, so as to remind you again, because of the grace that was given me from God, to be a minister of Christ Jesus to the Gentiles, ministering as a priest the gospel of God, that my offering of the Gentiles might become acceptable, sanctified by the Holy Spirit.* — Romans 15:15-16

Part of the fallen nature of man results in the tendency for one people to regard themselves as superior to others who aren't equipped with the "proper" skin color, nationality, education, social standing, athletic ability, or whatever. Indeed, we are all different in terms of appearance, abilities, knowledge, habits, preferences, and so on. God made us that way. In his economy, none of that really matters.

"Men of low degree are only vanity, and men of rank are a lie. In the balances they go up. They are together lighter than breath" (Psalm 62:9).

What does matter is that we are equal in value to God. Christ died for all of us. Realizing that, Paul, a Jew, became an effective minister of Christ to the Gentiles.

If anyone should be demonstrating to the world how people of difference can work together in harmony, it is God's people. We do it, not because it is politically correct, but because the Lord Jesus Christ is our great common denominator.

And along the way, we just might make an interesting discovery. When we give different people a chance, we not only help them, but we find that they have much they can teach us.

---

**Characters:** (young ladies around age sixteen)
The Pacesetters
    Jerri
    Terri
    Kerri
    Mary
Sue — the new person

*(The four Pacesetters are all wearing the same type and color of shirts. They enter at stage right doing some kind of precision drill. After about twenty seconds of this, they square up and do a slap-hand drill. Sue enters from stage right wearing a different kind of shirt and carrying a book. She walks past the other girls and goes to the other side of the stage where she sits down and begins to read. The four stop their slap-hand routine and begin to converse. Sue cannot hear them)*

**Jerri:** There goes Alice the Alien.

**Terri:** *(Derisively)* Look at that shirt.

**Kerri:** And she's reading a book!

**Jerri:** Give me a break. Nobody reads books anymore.

**Terri:** I wonder what she does for fun?

**Kerri:** Probably a lot of solitaire.

(*The three girls laugh*)

**Mary:** Maybe she needs some friends.

**Jerri:** You got that right. She's the least popular girl in school.

**Mary:** So why don't we decide to like her?

**Terri:** What? We're the Pacesetters. What would everyone think if we lowered ourselves to that? (*Points at Sue*)

**Mary:** Well, I'm going to talk to her.

**Kerri:** Not if you want to be one of us.

**Mary:** You wouldn't do that.

**Jerri:** Bet us.

(*Mary looks at her friends intently. Then she looks at Sue, sitting alone. She starts toward Sue and stops. She turns around, walks past the girls, and exits. The following line is uttered while she is walking past them*)

**Terri:** Having second thoughts?

(*Mary says nothing*)

**Kerri:** Freeze her out. Tomorrow she'll come begging to join us again.

(*Mary reenters, now wearing a shirt just like Sue's. The three watch speechlessly as she walks past them and heads over to Sue. They exit as soon as Mary begins speaking*)

**Mary:** Hi, I'm Mary.

**Sue:** (*Shyly*) I'm Sue.

**Mary:** I thought your name was Alice.

**Sue:** Nope. It's always been Sue.

**Mary:** What are you reading?

**Sue:** Oh, just an English class assignment, *The Hunchback of Notre Dame*. It's about a guy who was all weird and deformed, but who really had a heart of gold.

**Mary:** Do you have a lot of feeling for people who hurt?

**Sue:** My mom and dad run a home for abused and abandoned children. I help them on weekends doing puppet shows or wherever else they need my help.

**Mary:** You do puppet shows? I've always wanted to learn puppets.

**Sue:** Well, come over to my house after school. I'll teach you.

**Mary:** I'd love that. (*Looks at her watch*) I guess it's time to head for class. Where are you headed?

**Sue:** Mr. Kleehopper's U. S. History class.

**Mary:** I'm going that way. I'll walk with you. (*On the way out*) What kind of puppets do you do?

**Sue:** All kinds — and I make my own. I'll show you that, too.


## Discussion Questions:

1. Have you ever experienced being an outcast? What was the experience like?

2. Have you ever prejudged an individual who appeared different and then realized later how wrong you were?

3. What are some of the difficulties in reaching out to those who are different?

4. In what ways do we grow as people when we reach out to those who are different?

# 29. The Receptionist

*Greet Mary, who has worked hard for you.* — Romans 16:6

This sketch addresses one of the greatest of all human needs — the need for recognition and appreciation. Paul knew about it. His letters are filled with references to dear saints who weren't the most conspicuous people, but who were faithful servants of the Lord. Now here, in Romans, he devotes nearly the entire last chapter to recognizing such people, none of whom would have ever made it into any secular history book.

But don't we run the risk of giving people a big head? We run a greater risk of losing people if we don't show appreciation. It isn't our job to make sure people don't get puffed up by ignoring them. Why would Paul have devoted Romans 16 to recognizing people if it were wrong to do so?

---

**Characters:**
Mary — the receptionist
Pastor Burns — senior pastor
Pastor Danielovich — associate pastor
Bernadette — aerobics class instructor
Mary's husband
Various assorted extras

**Setting:**
The front desk at a large church. Mary is seated at the desk cluttered with paraphernalia. The phone is constantly ringing and people are coming at her from all directions with things for her to do. She is on the phone as this vignette begins.

(*Someone walks across the stage in front of Mary with a sign facing the audience that says "9 a.m."*)

**Mary:** I can't come home now, Tracy. See if Grandma can't stitch up your dolly. (*Pause*) Thanks, hon. (*Pause*) I'm 29.

**Pastor Burns:** Mary, I need you to run three copies of my Sunday sermon for the choir director, Pastor Danielovich, and for the elder board. (*Hands the sermon to her*)

**Mary:** I'll have them in the proper slots by two.

**Pastor Burns:** Thank you, Mary. (*The phone rings*)

**Mary:** Hillsdale Community Church. How may I direct your call? Oh, hi, Alice. (*Pause*) That's an interesting idea. (*The phone rings again*) I've got another call. Let me put you on hold. Hillsdale

Community Church. How may I direct your call? (*Pause*) I'm sorry you didn't like the message last Sunday. (*Pause*) That's what we believe here. (*Pause*) We don't respond well to threats, sir. Have a nice day. (*Clicks off that line*)

**Bernadette:** Mary, I've got to get these flyers for the next aerobics class printed up immediately.

**Mary:** I'll do my best, Bernadette. Hello, Alice? (*Pause*) I'll tell Pastor Burns about your idea. (*Pause*) Good, nice talking to you, too.

**Pastor Danielovich:** Mary, I need you to type up this letter for the missions board.

**Mary:** Is 5 p.m. soon enough?

**Pastor Danielovich:** That'll be fine. Thanks, Mary.

**Mary:** (*Dials the print shop extension*) Hello, Myrtle? Can you run off 500 copies of an aerobics class flyer for Bernadette today? (*Pause*) I'm not too well-schooled on that printer. (*Pause*) Okay, I'll be over at lunchtime. (*Hangs the phone up and has about five seconds of peace. She is showing a little fatigue. The phone rings*)
    Hillsdale Community Church. How may I direct your call? (*Pause*) Listen, don't do that. Let me make you an appointment with one of our pastors right away. (*Pause*) I know, but that's a very permanent solution to a temporary problem.

(*The sign holder comes across the stage with a sign saying "5 p.m." Mary now looks totally frazzled*)

**Pastor Burns:** Did you get those three sermon copies to where they belonged?

**Mary:** Yes, Pastor Burns. Alice Scruggs called. She says God told her to tell us to rent one of those advertising planes and have it pull a sign around the community saying, "WOE, OR GO TO HILLSDALE COMMUNITY CHURCH." She says the thought came to her from Revelation 8:13 in her devotions this morning.

**Pastor Burns:** Thanks for the message, Mary.

**Pastor Danielovich:** Do you have my letter ready for the missions board?

**Mary:** Yes, Pastor Danielovich. (*Hands it to him*)

**Pastor Danielovich:** Thank you, Mary.

**Bernadette:** Do you have those flyers ready?

**Mary:** Yes, Bernadette. They're at the print shop.

**Bernadette:** Great. I knew they would come through for me.

**Mary:** They do a good job.

(*Everyone exits and Mary is alone. She grabs her purse and wearily begins to exit. Suddenly, everyone who has appeared and others, including her family, emerge from every direction. All have gifts for her which they begin piling on her desk*)

**All:** Surprise!

(*They sing the Happy Birthday song, ending it with "And many more." Mary really perks up. She wasn't expecting this*)

**Mary:** I don't know what to say.

**Pastor Burns:** Mary, you are by far the best receptionist we have ever had.

**Mary's Husband:** Honey, it's all arranged. We're all going right now to the Pied Piper for a party in your honor.

(*Everybody picks up the gifts and they all go off together*)

## Discussion Questions:

1. Why is it important to give deserving people proper recognition?

2. Have you ever been recognized for some achievement? How did that recognition affect you?

3. When might recognition be a bad thing?

# 30. The Bully

*For the report of your obedience has reached to all; therefore I am rejoicing over you, but I want you to be wise in what is good, and innocent in what is evil. And the God of peace will soon crush Satan under your feet.*     — Romans 16:19-20

Question: What is the best way to battle Satan?
Answer:    To walk in close fellowship with God.

We who know the Lord Jesus Christ, whether we like it or not, are at war with the devil. It comes with the territory. It is a war that the devil cannot win (Matthew 25:41), but which we can personally lose if we don't do battle according to God's directions.

Just as the Roman soldier put on his armor before going into battle, so the Christian must put on the armor of God (Ephesians 6:10-18). If we determine to fight the battle without that armor, Satan will sift us like wheat (Luke 22:31-34). With the armor we always win (1 John 4:4).

Where do many of us go wrong? I believe it often comes from a tendency to study evil with the intent of attacking it, while subtly drifting away from vital fellowship with God. Evil has a natural fascination. Pride creeps into the picture (Matthew 26:33-35). Before we know it, we are like the police officer in the inner city who spends so much time fighting the drug scene that he becomes hooked himself.

Is the solution naivete? No. We are not to be ignorant of Satan's schemes (2 Corinthians 2:11).

Is the solution to stay indoors and never to venture out into battle? No. Jesus said, "I send you out as sheep in the midst of wolves; therefore be shrewd as serpents, and innocent as doves" (Matthew 10:16).

There is a way to put on the armor and walk with God; to do battle and not fall victim to the wiles of the devil. It does not mean we won't pay a heavy price for being God's warriors. "All who desire to live godly in Christ Jesus will be persecuted" (2 Timothy 3:12). But though we might get knocked around, we'll never be knocked out (2 Corinthians 4:7-12).

In the following sketch, Quincy has so filled his life with junk, that he is powerless to withstand the blows of the enemy. Darla, by contrast, has chosen the good part. This is a flesh and blood illustration of the real spiritual war that is being waged every day in our lives.

---

**Characters:**
Quincy — the wimp
Darla — the girl
Snake — the bully

**Setting:**
A "romantic" hillside.

**Darla:** So why did you bring me up here, Quincy?

**Quincy:** I just thought it might be the best place to tell you what's in my heart. Look at the view.

**Darla:** Great view of the junkyard below. And there's the county prison over there, and over that way is the city dump and the cement factory.

**Quincy:** I have a gift for you. (*Hands her a gift box*)

**Darla:** (*Opens the box and takes out a battery-powered croaking frog*) Ummm, thanks, Quincy. Very nice.

**Quincy:** Darla, oh, Darla. (*Takes her by the hand*)

(*The Bully enters from stage left*)

**Quincy:** Since the day I first saw you coming out of Thrifty's, I just knew you were the ...

**Bully:** Hi, squirt.

**Quincy:** Are you addressing me?

**Bully:** Don't see any other squirts around here. Hey, you're a sweet babe. (*Takes Darla by her free hand*)

**Quincy:** Unhand her, or I'll ...

**Bully:** You'll what? (*Lets go of Darla's hand and grasps Quincy's shirt under his chin with his left hand*)

**Quincy:** I'll (*Pause*) file a formal protest.

**Bully:** Yeah! Well, I'm shaking in my boots. (*Raises his right hand in a fist and bonks it down on top of Quincy's head. Quincy collapses in a heap*)
    They call me Snake. Come on, babe. A girl like you deserves a real man — like me. (*Grabs her hand. She jerks it from him*)
    Hey now. I'm just a friendly guy.

(*He moves again toward her. She assumes a martial arts stance and delivers five different blows with her verbal karate sound effects. The fifth blow KO's him. Then she helps Quincy up*)

**Quincy:** How did you do that?

**Darla:** (*As they are exiting off stage*) Been going to (*whatever hard-core disciplesh program you have that more of your people ought to be involved in*). You ought to start coming, too.

## Discussion Questions:

1. Why was Quincy so weak?

2. How was Darla so strong?

3. Is staying indoors and never venturing into the battle the safest place for the Christian to be?

4. If a Christian properly puts on the full armor of God, is he invulnerable to being hurt in the battle?

# Music for Sketch 13 — The New Creation

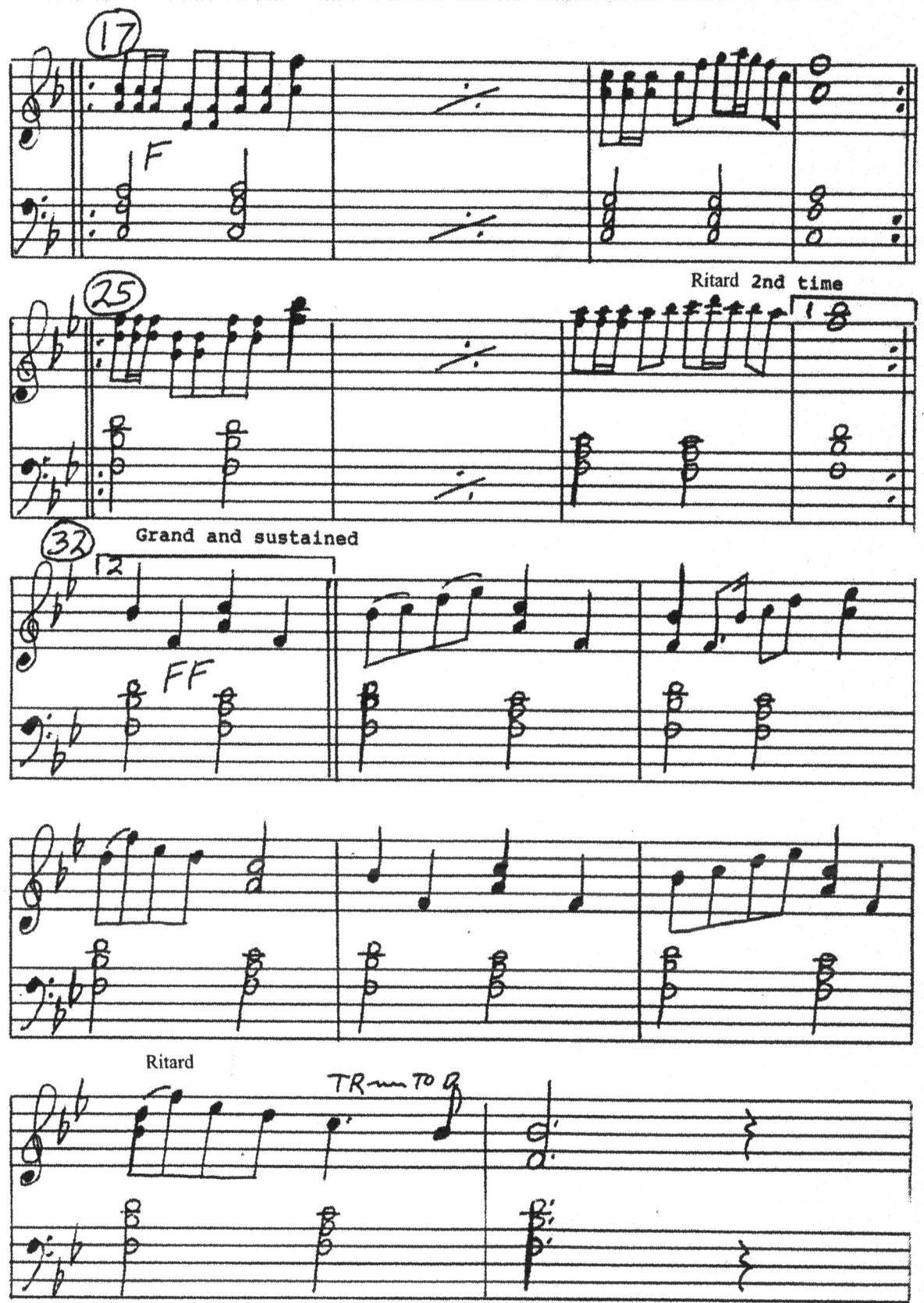

# Music for Sketch 18 — The Marionette
## "Minuet" (from the Notebook of Anna Magdelena Bach) — Bach

# Music for Sketch 22 — The Flower
*From "The William Tell Overture" — Rossini*

# Music for Sketch 22 — The Flower
*From "Les Sylphides" — Chopin*

www.ingramcontent.com/pod-product-compliance
Lightning Source LLC
Chambersburg PA
CBHW082235170426
43196CB00041B/2799